The Man They Couldn't Hang

*A Tale of
Murder, Mystery and Celebrity*

Michael Crowley

A play in two acts with an introduction by the author

The Man They Couldn't Hang

A Tale of Murder, Mystery and Celebrity

Michael Crowley

A play in two acts with an introduction by the author

Published 2010 by
Waterside Press
Sherfield Gables
Sherfield on Loddon
Hook, Hampshire
United Kingdom RG27 0JG

Telephone +44(0)1256 882250
Low cost UK landline calls
0845 2300 733
E-mail
enquiries@watersidepress.co.uk
Online catalogue
WatersidePress.co.uk

ISBN 9781904380 641 (Paperback)

Copyright © 2010 This work is the copyright of Michael Crowley. All intellectual property and associated rights are hereby asserted and reserved by the author in full compliance with UK, European and international law. No part of this book may be copied, reproduced, stored in any retrieval system or transmitted in any form or by any means, including in hard copy or via the internet, without the prior written permission of the publishers to whom all such rights have been assigned.

Cataloguing-In-Publication Data A catalogue record for this book can be obtained from the British Library.

Cover design © 2010 Waterside Press. Hangman illustration by Meg Veale (www.MegVeale.com).

UK distributor Gardners Books, 1 Whittle Drive, Eastbourne, East Sussex, BN23 6QH. Tel: +44 (0)1323 521777; sales@gardners.com; gardners.com

North American distributor International Specialised Book Services (ISBS), 920 NE 58th Ave, Suite 300, Portland, Oregon, 97213-3786, USA
Tel: 1 800 944 6190 Fax 1 503 280 8832 orders@isbs.com www.isbs.com

e-book *The Man They Couldn't Hang* is available as an ebook (e-book ISBN 9781906534974) and also to subscribers of Myilibrary and Dawsonera.

Printed by the MPG Books Group, Bodmin and King's Lynn.

The Man They Couldn't Hang

*A Tale of
Murder, Mystery and Celebrity*

Michael Crowley

A play in two acts with an introduction by the author

☆ WATERSIDE PRESS

One of the most enduring and acclaimed works for people using drama-based approaches with offenders or other groups.

The Geese Theatre Handbook
Drama with Offenders and People at Risk
by Clark Baim, Sally Brookes and Alun Mountford

Geese Theatre UK is renowned in criminal justice circles. Members of the company perform issue-based plays and hold workshops in prisons, young offender institutions, probation centres and similar settings. The company has worked in virtually every prison and each probation area in the UK and Ireland—and also works with youth justice teams. A perennial best-seller *The Geese Theatre Handbook* explains the thinking behind the company's approach.

- Contains **100+ exercises with explanations, instructions and suggestions**
- Helps practitioners develop their own style and approach
- Materials can be readily adapted to other settings including conflict resolution, restorative justice and interpersonal skills training

'A generous book [which] provides a treasure chest of games and exercises for any group setting ... a wealth of food for thought ... for trainers of all kinds ... an invaluable addition to the Waterside list': ***Criminal Justice Matters***. 'An invaluable resource': ***Prison Service News***. 'Fascinating ... Excellent ... If you're involved with offenders or other risk groups, buy it': ***The Magistrate***. 'An absolute treasure trove for people who work with groups–in mental health, schools, training, social work–wherever': ***Mental Health Today***.

223 pp | 08/03/2002 | Paperback ISBN 9781872870670 | Ebook ISBN 9781906534509

Contents

About the Author   *vi*
Introduction   *vii*
Further Reading   *xvi*
Cast of Characters   *xvii*

ACT I *19*

Scene One...*21*
Scene Two *47*
Scene Three *53*
Scene Four *63*
Scene Five *83*
Scene Six *97*

ACT II *103*

Scene Seven..*105*
Scene Eight *113*
Scene Nine...*123*
Scene Ten...*127*
Scene Eleven *133*
Scene Twelve *143*

On Being a Writer in Residence in a Prison.................. *151*

About the Author

Michael Crowley is a writer and youth justice worker who has written for stage, radio and film. His first play 'Beyond Omarska' was produced by Box of Tricks Theatre and shortlisted for the BBC's Alfred Bradley Bursary Award and The Kings Cross Award. He has written for youth and community theatre and was writer in residence at HM Prison and Young Offender Institution Lancaster Farms between 2007 and 2010. 'The Man They Couldn't Hang' is his second full length play. He lives in West Yorkshire.

Introduction

The Man They Couldn't Hang

Michael Crowley

This story found its way to me with the death of my friend's grandfather. He came back from the funeral, we went to the pub and he told me his memories of the man. One of them was of his grandfather telling him, that as a child, he had seen The Man They Couldn't Hang on stage describing his ordeal on the gallows. John 'Babbacombe' Lee had stood in convict attire, replete with chains, recounting his own execution. Suffice to say that it stayed with the Edwardian child to the end of his long life. I knew nothing of the story then; of its great potency. E. M. Forster said that 'story can only have one merit; that of wanting the audience to know what happens next'. And I wanted to know; about the aftermath, and about the twist of fate that had brought John Lee to the gallows in the first place. So I spent the next day at Manchester's Central Reference Library.

Here was a story with all the components of great crime fiction. It felt like the stencil for the board game Cluedo. The murder took place in a Country House in a remote location; the victim was a wealthy, elderly, devout lady; the perpetrator, her poor and unhappy servant; the method of murder, grisly.

John Lee was a humble servant who was considered guilty even before he'd reached the court where he wasn't permitted to speak in his own defence. It was class justice and when the guilty verdict was pronounced, the cynical remark of 'The butler did it' was coined in pubs across the country as a judgement on the kind of justice a servant could expect. Here was a sensational murder and trial. What my friend's grandfather had seen on stage was in real life supported by an ensemble cast: the inept and vainglorious hangman; a callous but stunned Home Secretary and The Abolitionists. It was depicted in Sunday newspaper exclusives and became the subject of book deals. Music hall impresarios sought to cash in on Divine Providence. If the dreadful murder of Emma Keyse was the prototype of the Victorian crime, the case of The Man They Couldn't Hang became the black and white negative of the murderer turned celebrity.

John Lee was the son of a clay miner. He began his working life at the scene of the crime, The Glen, when he was fourteen-years-old. The Glen was a spacious marine villa near Babbacombe in Devon, built in 1812 on a 13 acre estate. The owner was a Miss Emma Ann Keyse, unmarried but accompanied by her servants. Crucial to the story, it seems, is the necessity for Emma Keyse to sell the house from the moment she inherited it. Within a year of his first stint at The Glen, John Lee left to join the Royal Navy. This was the first of his many failed attempts to escape his background, for he was discharged on the grounds of ill-health within two years. He returned to South Devon and Miss Keyse considerately used her influence to find him a position as a footman to a Colonel Brownlow in Torquay. It was a living, but one he was obviously at variance with and within a year he was arrested for trying to pawn the Brownlow family sliver. This was an ill-thought out caper for which he appeared at Exeter Assizes where he was sentenced to six months' hard labour. Hence, the central character in this real-life drama acquired form.

Again Emma Keyse came to his aid. She now took him in as her footman, reuniting him with his half-sister Lizzie Harris who was cook at The Glen. Twenty-year-old John Lee had a uniform, a pantry to sleep in near Lizzie and two shillings and sixpence a week. Before long he had a sweetheart, Kate Farmer, who became his fiancée. Then within weeks of the engagement, a buyer appeared for the estate and the servants' positions were placed in jeopardy, none more so than the new, ex-convict footman. John Lee, it seems, flew into a rage, such that the charitable Emma Keyse admonished him by reducing his wages to two shillings week; less than a man could live on. His engagement to Kate Farmer was called off. Faced with the full impotency of his situation he burst into Lizzie's kitchen and told her he 'would have his revenge…lay the place in ashes.'[1]

Two weeks later in the early hours of Saturday morning, November 15th, 1884, Emma Keyse's body was found by her servants in the dining room, lacerated and on fire. It had been dragged from the hall then set alight with paraffin to accelerate the blaze:

> The throat was cut. All the main arteries being severed…Even the parietal bone was notched…There [were] also wounds from burning, the right foot being much charred and also one hand…The blows must have been occasioned by a round instrument, a kind of hammer. The wounds on the deceased's throat would have completely drawn the body of blood in a few minutes.[2]

There had been an act of explosive violence followed by a bungled attempt to cover it up. John Lee went to the village to summon assistance and was arrested on his return.

The excitement about the murder was soon widespread. Technology was revolutionizing newspapers. Telegraph lines had been laid across the oceans and they were employed to send the gory details to the *New York Herald* and *The Toronto Globe*.[3] The initial spotlight was a flavour of what was to come.

---

[1] Deposition of Elizabeth Harris to Coroner's Inquest, 19.November 1884, Torquay Police Court. Public Record Office, Kew, English Assize Record reference; ASSI/262164326.

[2] Deposition of Nicholas Chilcote, Surgeon. (Ibid)

[3] *The Secret of the Babbacombe Murder* (1995), Mike Holgate, Peninsula Press, p.19.

Whilst the press had an insatiable appetite for the trial of John Lee, the Victorian legal system excluded him from participating in the proceedings. Four days after the murder a coroner's inquest resulted in a verdict of wilful murder against him. It was an inquest at which he was not present, yet it committed him for trial on charges of murder and arson; a trial at which he was not permitted to speak. Witnesses at the inquest described how his clothes smelt of oil, and of how his arm was cut and a hatchet found near where he slept. Lizzie's evidence of her step-brother's threats was damming. When it came to the trial itself, his lawyer withdrew two days before it started on the grounds of ill-health. He sent his inexperienced 22-year-old brother to defend Lee against an accomplished member of Queen's Counsel. The blood and oil on John Lee's clothing, he argued, were from putting out the fire on the body; the cut on his arm from breaking a window to let out the smoke. The jury took less than 40 minutes to return with a verdict of guilty. John Lee calmly protested his innocence then was sentenced to hang.

The evidence against John Lee was circumstantial, but it was in abundance. Matches similar to those found scattered around the body were also found in his coat pocket. The threats he made to Lizzie he had also repeated to the postman. The kernel of his defence was that no murderer would have been so stupid as to lay such a trail of self-incriminating evidence. But murderers rarely think like lawyers.

There was, however, one line of circumstantial evidence that was only tentatively pursued at trial, a line that the murder history detectives have been chasing-up ever since, and that concerns Lizzie. Late night visitors to the servant's quarters at The Glen were common, especially on a Friday. Unmarried Lizzie was three months pregnant at the trial. Whilst the identity of the father was never confirmed, it was rumoured to be Gwynne Templer, John Lee's errant lawyer. These two tiny threads and John's lifetime pleas of innocence, have led some people to argue that the wrong man was convicted. Lizzie was also reputed to have made a deathbed confession from the workhouse. But none of this would ever have been dragged into the light without what happened next.

Execution by hanging in Britain's Victorian jails was outsourced. Advertisements or notices for forthcoming executions were placed in newspapers and suitably qualified applicants (or as it sometimes transpired not so suitably qualified ones) wrote to the local sheriff offering their services. Of course, after a little experience one could build up a solid CV and expect to earn a good living. One such freelancer was Bradford born ex-policeman James Berry, at this time only a year into the job but already with 13 men and two women under his belt.

Berry's very first application to perform an execution was turned down after his mother was so appalled by her son's choice of a new career that she wrote to the Aldermen of the City of London imploring them not to give James the tender. For a short while, the work went to a character called Binns. He invariably turned up drunk at executions, occasioning disastrous results, and when prohibited from further appointments, the path was open for Berry.

Berry also drank, both before and after executions and not surprisingly eventually became an alcoholic. He admitted that he was drawn to the work by the money but did at least attempt a scientific-cum-scholarly approach to the role. He came to write and lecture extensively about his work, his methods and his subjects, eventually publishing *Memoirs of an Executioner*. Self-regarding even in autobiographical terms, the opening chapter is entitled 'The Executioner at Home'. Berry eventually became well-known in Victorian society and openly sought celebrity status. By the time he was forbidden by the Home Office from tendering for any more executions, he owned six houses and was appearing at theatres with his slide shows and telling jokes, for a fee. The

'John Babbacombe Lee job' undoubtedly helped propel him onto the stage.

The gallows at Exeter Prison had been specially built for the execution in question; a job that involved the labour of prisoners. Berry arrived on the Saturday and found the trap doors to be working satisfactorily. On the Monday at the appointed time he went to John Lee's cell and shook his hand. Then he slipped a belt around his waist, buckled it and strapped the condemned man's arms to it. His wrists were also strapped near the buckle. Then a procession of chief warder, chaplain, John Lee, warder, Berry the executioner, the prison Governor and Under Sheriff made their way to the scaffold, with a prison bell tolling. As they walked, the chaplain read The Burial Service. When they reached the gallows, inside a shed, Lee was placed on the trap doors and his legs were tied.

From the trial onwards many of those involved remarked on the composure of John Lee. The judge himself commented on the defendant's calmness, to which Lee replied: 'The reason, my Lord, why I am so calm and collected is because I trust in the Lord, and He knows I am innocent.' Shortly before his execution his mother described him as unconcerned about his fate, 'as if he were going to the theatre.'[4]

Berry drew the white cap over John's head and tightened the noose.

'Have you anything to say?'

'No. Drop away.'

They waited for the chaplain to finish the service. Then Berry pulled the lever to release the drop but the doors just sagged a

---

4 Holgate. (p.24)

couple of inches. John supported himself on his toes whilst the warders and Berry stamped on the doors. A warder is reported as jumping on them but they would not open. Lee was dragged off the trap to one side. Berry then tested the lever without him and the trap doors opened. John was then dragged back onto the trap, the chaplain began reading once more, Berry pulled the lever and the doors failed again. The agony was inflicted for a third time before the chaplain fainted and the whole thing was called off for the time being.

Lee was prayed for in Exeter churches the Sunday before and a crowd had gathered outside the jail waiting for the black flag to be hoisted. Instead, reporters dashed out spreading the news of a miracle. Within an hour the news was in London and questions were being asked in the House of Commons the same night.

With the personal intervention of the Queen, John Lee's sentence was commuted to life imprisonment. Home Secretary Sir William Harcourt ordered that he be kept at Her majesty's pleasure. He ended up serving 22 years when the average life term was 15. A lot of it was hard labour and eight months of it was in solitary confinement. Sir William Harcourt knew both Emma Keyse and Colonel Brownlow. Lee even claimed that he had waited upon him at Colonel Brownlow's. He described prison as being taken 'from one tomb to another'.[5]

There has been more conjecture about the gallows than the murder. It had rained all through the Sunday and one theory is that the boards simply swelled under John's weight and stuck. Another is that the bolt was too long for the purpose; years later one of the prisoners who constructed the gallows claimed to have constructed it to operate as such. There was also talk about Berry being bribed and of course witchcraft and Divine Intervention.

---

[5] *The Man They Couldn't Hang* (1908), John Lee, republished by Devon Books.

Whatever the actual cause, the 'cock up' was given meaning by the populace.

People petitioned for John's cause. A music hall impresario offered to put him on stage upon his release. When the day finally came he was greeted by a crowd at Torquay Railway Station and journalists were waiting for him at his home village of Abbottskerwell. A Penny Dreadful was published to coincide with his release and his story was also serialised in a Sunday newspaper for a fee rumoured to be four thousand pounds.[6] The serialisation was republished in book form in 1908 and became a best-seller.

By the time of John Lee's release, James Berry's career as a hangman was over; there had been one too many bungled executions including a decapitation. Within days of his dismissal he was booked into the Imperial Theatre London as a 'Phrenologist and Character Reader'. He showed slides depicting dungeons and torture, swords used in executions, personal belongings taken from subjects and told tales from his exploits, including of course, about John Babbacombe Lee. He made a number of appearances around the country but his career as a performer was short lived. At some point alcoholism, or unpopularity, got the better of him. Berry eventually joined The Temperance Movement, one of several conversions. He also advocated for The Abolitionists and became an evangelical preacher after breaking the sixth commandment on a hundred and thirty four occasions. Berry always wanted to be a personality, a celebrity. He pursued it down several avenues, but who would warm to him?

Conversely, fame pursued John Lee for the rest of his life and beyond. The Home Secretary had to make it a condition of his release licence that he 'shall not take part in any public perfor-

---

[6] Holgate. (p.30)

mance or deliver any lecture or speech, or in any way exhibit himself at any meeting, assembly, or pace of entertainment'.[7]

Undoubtedly the authorities were worried by the macabre prospect of the double act of Lee and Berry, reunited on stage. They may well have also been concerned about John being enlisted by The Abolitionists. The licence condition was circumvented by John being employed as a barman in London and his first wife, who he soon abandoned, told the Relief Board in Lambeth that he received a salary for 'exhibiting himself'. [8] There was a silent film made of the story and some claim that he made personal appearances before screenings in the early twenties

In all likelihood it was an actor that my friend's grandfather saw as a child. There could only ever be one John Babbacombe Lee and so far as anybody knows he chose obscurity leaving England for America in 1911. But it is such a potent story we all want to believe that there is something in it.

The music hall impresario who tried to reunite the old double act of Lee and Berry is thought to have been a former music hall memory man William Bottell, also known as Datas. A character based upon him appears in the 1959 film version of The Thirty Nine Steps with the catchphrase 'Am I right sir?' Although his idea for a bizarre music hall turn was effectively banned, who's to say they never rehearsed?

---

[7] Holgate (p.32)

[8] Holgate (p. 33)

Further Reading

The Secret of the Babbacombe Murder (1995), Mike Holgate, Peninsula Press.

The Man They Couldn't Hang (1908), John Lee, republished by Devon Books.

The Babbacombe Murder (1988), Frank Keyse, Carreg Lwyd.

Executioner. The Chronicles of James Berry, Victorian Hangman (2004), Stewart P. Evans, Sutton Publishing.

Cast of Characters

The play takes place in a music hall in Leeds in 1907.

The Characters

Douglas Fawcett	Owner of a small and struggling music hall in Leeds. Early fifties.
Henry Cheetham	A music hall agent. Mid thirties.
Evelyn Nesbitt	Douglas's mistress and a music hall act, early forties.
James Berry	A retired hangman.
John Lee	An ex convict. Forty two years old.

Up stage left there is a music hall manager's office with a desk, chairs either side. The music hall is past its best and belongs more to the nineteenth century, from whence it hasn't progressed. There may be bills posted of peculiar acts that have played at Fawcett's Music Hall: 'Mephisto The Man Snake; Dario the Demon Trick Cyclist; Lillie Little and Her Singing Poodle'. Stage right and down stage centre is used to represent rehearsal and performance space, as well as other settings.

N.B. A slash "/" marks the point in a line of dialogue where the following line overlaps.

'All that is solid melts into air, all that is holy is profaned, and man is at last compelled to face with sober senses his real condition of life and his relations with his kind':

Karl Marx, *Manifesto of the Communist Party*, 1848.

'Never overestimate the intelligence of the public':

Don Simpson, Hollywood Producer.

Act I

Scene One

Lights lift on Evelyn singing out to her audience. Slightly upstage right, Douglas plays the piano. The office is in darkness. Evelyn is dressed in a dark skirt and a white blouse of the period; Douglas in a tweed jacket. These are not performance outfits but the number is sung with all the conviction of a performance. 'Let Me Call You Sweetheart', (words by Beth Slater Whitson music by Leo Friedman), a melancholy love song.

> I am dreaming, dear, of you day by day
> Dreaming when the skies are blue
> When they're grey
> When the silvery moon light gleams,
> Still I wander on in dreams,
> In a land of love, it seems, just with you
>
> Let me call you sweetheart I'm in love with you
> Let me hear you whisper that you love me too
> Keep the love-light glowing
> In your eyes so true
> Let me call you sweetheart
> I'm in love with you.
> Longing for you all the while
>
> More and more
> Longing for the sunny smile I adore
> Birds are singing far and near
> Roses blooming everywhere,
> You alone my heart can cheer
> You just you

> Let me call you sweetheart I'm in love with you
> Let me hear you whisper that you love me too
> Keep the love light glowing
> In your eyes so true
> Let me call you sweetheart
> I'm in love with you.

The lights change to general and Evelyn turns and approaches Douglas casually. This is a rehearsal of new songs.

Douglas: What diya think?

Evelyn: I do like it.

Douglas: We'll have it in yer turn by weekend.

Pause — one beat.

Evelyn: Not sure though.

Douglas: What aren't you sure about?

Evelyn: It's a bit ... unhappy

Douglas: How can it be? Love song.

Evelyn: She's got her head in the clouds.

Douglas: She's in the throes of romance.

Evelyn: She could be wasting her time though.

Douglas: What? Look they've just met. Not meant to be serious Evelyn. Let me buy it for yer. You made it sound beautiful.

Evelyn looks at the other sheet music on the piano.

Evelyn: What else have you got here?

Douglas: I don't reckon much to the others.

Evelyn: Don't be mean Duggie

Douglas: Not a question of mean.

Evelyn: What is it then?

Douglas: None of them's you. Throw your audience with too many new songs.

Evelyn: Audience know all me songs. Been singing them for years. What about this one?

Douglas: You're not doin' bawdy

Evelyn: I don't mind. 'Where Did Robinson Crusoe Go with Friday on a Saturday Night?'

Douglas: Not to my flamin' music hall. You're a romantic performer. Try it a few more times. I have some book keeping to do. We'll have supper eh?

They kiss.

Evelyn: You look tired Duggie.

Douglas: Aye.

Evelyn: Maybe we should get some fresh air. Whitby next weekend. What diya say?

Douglas: I'd love to.

Evelyn: I bet yer would

Douglas: I can't.

Evelyn: No

Douglas: Short of turns again.

Evelyn: Why don't we go to the pier in Scarborough, see some?

Douglas: In a few weeks we will.

Evelyn: I might go myself. See if they need one.

Douglas: Evelyn

Evelyn: I quite fancy a change

Douglas: I'd like nothing more than a few days away.

Evelyn: It's not as if Gladys doesn't know, is it?

Douglas: No, it's not.

Evelyn: May as well bring her along if she's lonely.

Douglas: I'm in bother with the bank.

Evelyn: That's nothing new.

Douglas: Manager is. He wants results.

Evelyn: How long?

Douglas: End of the month. If I could just get straight here …

Enter Henry with James Berry. He sits Berry downstage outside the office.

Evelyn: You're a bit of a turn yourself Duggie.

Henry: I was just passing

Douglas: How sociable.

Evelyn: I wish you would.

Evelyn: You're looking well Evelyn. Isn't she Douglas?

Douglas: I'm busy Henry.

Henry: Of course Duggie. Very busy meself these days. Thought I'd drop by though.

Evelyn: How are you, Henry?

Henry: In the pink me. *(To Evelyn)* Still top of the bill I see.

EVELYN: Douglas has bought me a new song.

HENRY: And so he should. *(To Douglas)* Eh I saw that new girl of yours' the other night. The French one … Clarice.

DOUGLAS: Cla-reece

HENRY: Aye.

EVELYN: From Dewsbury

HENRY: She can wiggle a bit. Useful voice too.

DOUGLAS: Plays to the gallery.

HENRY: Fine pair of lungs on her. Is she represented?

DOUGLAS: Aye, by me.

HENRY: Shame. You're not looking for an agent are yer Evelyn?

EVELYN: No need.

HENRY: Douglas looking after you alright is he?

EVELYN: When I want to retire Henry, I'll send you a telegram and you can put me on your books. In the meantime, I think I fancy a change of air.

Exit Evelyn.

HENRY: Eh people are getting desperate for acts yer know.

Douglas: For your acts?

Henry: There's a lot of demand for my acts.

Douglas: Not surprised, I'd like to get me hands on one or two of them.

Henry: I'm on me way down to City Varieties now, as it happens.

Douglas: Is that so?

Henry: Aye.

Douglas: Well don't let me stop yer then.

Henry: Right, can I just use yer karzee?

Douglas: No you can't. Occupied. Got your career in it. Mine n all. Except you're too stupid to realise.

Henry: That's where you're wrong Douglas. And that's why I'm on me way to Varieties. I've got an act outside. Right now.

Douglas: That's about as near as he'll get.

Henry: I saw your bill outside. And I thought, this music hall needs new blood. I can help.

Douglas: The last act you helped me with, was Beaman's /Flying Funsters.

Henry Flying Funsters. Still out there Douglas.

Douglas: Charlatans, both of yer. Name like that, punters expect a trapeze act. What do we get from you? Pigeons.

Henry: Comedy pigeons.

Douglas: Didn't make me laugh.

Henry: Beautifully painted they were.

Douglas: Aye so was the dressing room. Don't want animals. Nowt but a cheap circus act.

Henry: Not cheap Duggie. Animals a'not cheap. There's a Kangaroo in London on hundred pound a week.

Douglas: He'll have a proper agent.

Henry: Beats me how he spends it all.

Douglas: I need acts Henry. But I can't afford good acts. So I need talent. This is a hall where people make a mark.

Henry: And I have just the man.

Douglas: Chances are he'll be on his way out, or we've seen it all before.

Henry: That's where you're wrong. He's new. And he's different. Five minutes of your time. That's all I'm asking.

Douglas: Why? You don't have good acts you never have. You have stupid acts. Yer half the reason this hall's in the state it's in.

HENRY: You haven't seen my portfolio have yer?

DOUGLAS: You've several highly unusual much sought after turns

HENRY: How did you know that?

DOUGLAS: Remember that mind reading duck you were promoting last year? *(Pause)* Why don't you jack it in Henry? Earn a living. Fact is, we're both gonna have to soon, rate this place is losing money. No room for us in Leeds. Here, *(Pressing a coin into Henry's hand)* buy the gullible sod outside a drink.

Henry makes for the door but turns to give it one last try.

HENRY: You've made one stupid mistake after another you have. Invested all wrong, for years. New seating, flock wallpaper, new karzies for the middle classes. But you didn't get them the acts. Then you end up in hock to that brewery. Your beer cost more than at the Palace. That pushed out the working man. You've not run this place well at all. So don't blame me. I've been a friend to this music hall, I have. I thought you were a friend to me,

DOUGLAS: Alright Henry

HENRY: Maybe/I've been mistaken

DOUGLAS: I'll see him

HENRY: all these years

DOUGLAS: Henry, I'll see him!

Douglas makes his way to the back stage office area. Henry follows.

Sit down. *(He pours out two drinks from a whisky bottle he has in the drawer)* Truth is I could do with a new act or two. Bills I've had lately.

HENRY: I've heard.

DOUGLAS: Can't afford the acts because the punters aren't coming so I've no money to turn it round. Performers these days. Nobody's in it for the love.

HENRY: Music hall's not a factory. I've always said that.

DOUGLAS: Maybe it's time I got out. All these laws now. Music Hall's lost its magic. People took chances when we first started. Do you remember Harry Norton?

HENRY: The Human Aquarium..?

DOUGLAS: Very same. Closed down.

HENRY: No!?

DOUGLAS: Cruelty to animals.

HENRY: Everything came back up.

DOUGLAS: Audiences now, fed on a plain diet. And picture houses opening everywhere.

Pause — one beat

How's your Lucy?

HENRY: Randy as ever. How's Gladys?

Pause — one beat.

DOUGLAS: Demanding–in all the wrong ways.

HENRY: And what about you and … ?

DOUGLAS: Wants me to make an honest woman of her.

HENRY: Difficult times. I'll fetch him in. You'll need to be a bit broadminded here.

DOUGLAS: I'm having a drink with you aren't I?

Henry walks over to where Berry is sitting and beckons him into Douglas's office. Berry hurriedly puts the hipflask away and walks over carrying his executioner's case.

HENRY: May I present, the very next lucrative attraction. Mr James Berry.

Douglas does not shake hands. He merely gazes at Berry who does not strike him as the entertaining type.

DOUGLAS: So you're interested in a career in music hall Mr Berry?

BERRY: I think I would be of interest to the paying public

DOUGLAS: Really?

BERRY: I do not sing or juggle, but Mr Cheetham tells me that I could hold the attention of an audience. For a spell.

DOUGLAS: What is it that you do then? Show me your act?

BERRY: I'm afraid it is not possible to demonstrate my vocation to you immediately sir

DOUGLAS: Why's that?

Pause–two beats

HENRY: He's a hangman.

DOUGLAS: A hangman! What kind of act is that? We can't bloody hang people on stage … .Can we?

BERRY: I'm retired. I hanged a hundred and thirty four, men and women.

HENRY: An executioner.

BERRY: My business card.

He takes a card from his pocket hands it to Douglas

DOUGLAS: You must be desperate Henry.

HENRY: Admit it Duggie, it's different.

Douglas: It's morbid. So if you don't hang people no more, what yer gonna do?

Berry: I can tell people tales bout my experiences as an executioner.

Douglas: That's not gonna make people laugh though is it?

Berry: People are usually interested. Excited even.

Henry: It's a different type of entertainment. A new type. Plays on a different emotion.

Douglas: Disgust.

Henry: We can sell it.

Berry: I appreciate your reservations Mr Fawcett. The proprietor of the City Varieties was also sceptical

Pause — one beat

Henry: Well at first he was …

Douglas: You've been misinformed Mr Berry

Gives him his card back.

Berry: I am sorry for wasting your time sir.

Berry picks up his case and shakes Douglas's hand and whilst he is still holding it …

HENRY: Before we go. What sort of drop would he require?

BERRY: Mr Fawcett?

Berry will not let go of Douglas's hand and is assessing his weight. He examines Douglas's frame closely.

He looks like an eight foot drop at least. Maybe nine, but

He approaches Douglas, drops his case and puts his hand upon Douglas's shoulders.

He is quite a muscular man. You were once physically active.

DOUGLAS: I was a hod carrier. Before he were born.

BERRY: I would select for you, my finest Italian silk hemp

Douglas is a little confused because he can't quite believe what is happening. Berry opens his case and brings out his hangman's noose. He shows it proudly to Douglas

I had a brass ring fitted to secure the noose. Behind the left ear. But first…

He hands it to Douglas, who examines the brass ring, whilst Berry delves into his case. Berry withdraws a white cap and the following happens too quickly for Douglas to resist.

the executioner must swiftly and skillfully cover the criminal's head with a white hood, *(He does so)* mercifully shutting from his view the last preparatory measures. The executioner's assistant *(He beckons Henry as of he were a magician's assistant)* pinions his legs *(Henry does this)* At last the noose is placed over the head, and with everything ready, both officials step back and with a quick action the executioner reaches for the lever /sending the condemned ...

Douglas begins to struggle.

DOUGLAS: What yer bloody doin man?

Douglas pulls off his noose and cap, unsettled.

I get the idea.

Henry unties his legs. Berry puts his equipment back into his case.

BERRY: Over the years I have managed to carry out these matters so speedily that the time occupied from the moment I enter the condemned cell, to the falling of the prisoner into the pit, is less than one minute.

DOUGLAS: You must be very proud of yourself

BERRY: My method of execution is the outcome of the experience of my predecessors. I am proud to say though, that I have made a modest contribution myself

DOUGLAS: Do tell us

HENRY: This is interesting

BERRY: The ascent to the scaffold was in the past made by series of steps. I found in some cases that criminals were nervous, even prostrated. The steps formed a practical difficulty. I suggested the substitution of a slope. A level gangway. In place of the steps.

DOUGLAS: Very considerate.

BERRY: The Home Office were grateful to me. First put to the test when I executed William Pritchard at Kirkdale Gaol April fifteen, eighteen ninety.

Berry takes out a number of photos from his jacket. He sorts through for Pritchard, hands it to Douglas.

DOUGLAS: One of your favourites?

BERRY: I have taken no pleasure in my art. I considered it a public duty.

Pause — one beat

While waiting for execution Pritchard frequently showed much emotion. I feared there might be a scene. But when the time came, he was composed. No reckless bravado, but a quiet submission.

Berry enters the spell of the moment.

He walks uprightly to the scaffold and stands motionless upon the drop. For a second his glance wanders round the prison yard and in this moment he seems to comprehend everything. He sees his grave ready dug in a corner — sobs a little. His only demonstration of feeling whilst in my hands.

Pause — one beat

Douglas: You remember them?

Berry: I meet them for a short while. But I observe how they die.

Douglas: So tell me Mr Berry, how come you no longer practice your art?

Berry: My livelihood was entirely uncertain. It depended upon the number of poor fellows condemned to die.

Douglas: Business falling off was it?

Berry: Everyman must obtain a living for his family.

Douglas: You think you'll do that in music hall?

Berry: My wife passed away many years ago, my children are grown.

Douglas: What makes you think the public will be interested?

Berry: Because certain newspapers claim to have interviewed me when I refuse to speak to them. When I travelled to a gaol for an appointment, I was forced to arrive by a train other than the one expected. Because when I am out in Bradford, I am stared at and followed about by the crowd — as if I were a monstrosity.

Pause–two beats

Douglas: Could you wait outside please, for a moment.

Berry returns to office exterior.

Henry: You can see the fascination. Don't lie to me you can see it.

Douglas: He wants to be liked. He never will be.

Henry: He wants to be on stage. Let him think he's liked.

Douglas: It's not performance

Henry: It's life. Well death. He knows about other types of execution. Got a big knife, were used to behead pirates in China.

Douglas: What's he gonna do?

Henry: What does it matter? It's what he used to do that people will want to know about. Look, bita music. Magic lantern show, elaborate effects, he talks and walks through his hangings.

Douglas: Becoming outdated lantern shows.

Henry: Get a gallows knocked up then.

Douglas: How much will that cost? ... Then what?

Henry: Berry brings members of the audience on stage, walks them up the steps, caps them, binds them, on with the noose ... and ...

Douglas: I've few enough in the audience as it is, without / hanging people …

Henry: No. They fall through the trap door, but the rope goes with them.

Pause — one beat. Douglas looks again at the photo he still has in his hand.

Douglas: Not sure I really approve of hanging

Henry: You believe in music hall don't you? How much is at stake here Douglas?

Douglas: Apart from my reputation

Henry: Reputation, integrity. They're only words. Berry's a five pound turn. He charged more than twice that to hang a man. Just to tell an audience how it felt though, he'll do it for next to nothing. And they'll want to know. He could save this place.

Douglas: Eh, I'm not so desperate you know.

Henry: Aren't yer? I was here when this place was just a shed. You could have walked away from it then. Not now. The bank 'll find you. Macabre bastard he may be but he could be the best profit margin you've had in years.

Douglas: He's something to put before interval. At best.

Henry: After

Douglas: A novelty.

Henry: You haven't seen him yet. I think he could go up the bill.

Douglas: Not what I call a turn though, someone talking about their occupation.

Henry: Not if you we're a hod carrier no. But he was Queen Victoria's executioner. Put this place in the papers.

Pause — one beat

Douglas: Haven't you got anyone else?

Henry: No. Not like him. But I will have if you put him on. We both will.

Douglas: Who?

Henry: Put him on and you'll find out. C'mon. You've not had a new act in months.

Douglas: Too pleased with himself. He's hung a hundred and thirty four people and now he wants a round of applause. What do you think?

Henry: About what?

Douglas: Hanging?

Henry: Never given much thought. Don't need an agent do yer. Though if they brought back public / hanging …

Douglas: Where does it end with you?

Henry: When punters won't pay. Now, any last words before you meet the executioner? Or don't you want to stick your neck out?

Henry walks down to centre stage to meet Berry. Douglas follows.

Douglas: You've never faced an audience have you Mr Berry? A music hall audience. You might have been worried about a mob when you went to hang someone, but if you don't have something to offer the mob in the stalls, they'll crucify you. So what is your act?

Berry looks to Henry for help

Henry: It's gonna need a bita tuning

Douglas: If you want me to put you on, I want to see it.

Berry: Well, I had thought that I might introduce myself and then provide the audience with a brief history of capital punishment.

Douglas: Then I'll wake em up shall I? Look, tell me what you remember most, from your hanging career?

Berry: Eh …

Douglas: Which hanging Mr Berry?

BERRY: January 1888. I hung Dr Philip Henry Eustace Cross. That was a highlight definitely.

DOUGLAS: Why?

BERRY: He was from an excellent family. A brave man.

DOUGLAS: It's no gentleman's club out there.

HENRY: Show him the sword

BERRY: I have some implements of interest.

Berry takes a scimitar shaped sword from his bag

This sword was used to behead nine men, successfully, with nine blows. I also have a garotting strap.

DOUGLAS: And what's the point of this?

BERRY: Well, there are those that believe that hanging is an unscientific form of capital punishment. I aim to show that it is by far the most humane method of execution.

DOUGLAS: It needs to be theatrical though. You need to do something.

HENRY: An assistant from the audience. Better still. Look.

Henry gets Douglas to kneel down as if he were about to be beheaded. Douglas is reluctant but Henry gets him to kneel.

DOUGLAS: What yer doin?

Henry: Well it can hardly be me can it? Conflict of interest.

Berry now hands Henry a black blindfold from his case. Henry blindfolds Henry. Meanwhile Berry consults a manuscript in his case.

Berry: "Apart from the fact that beheading under the best conditions is a revolting spectacle, we must further consider that because the executioner has to hack off the victim's head ...

Douglas looks up although he can't see obviously.

... he must therefore ... "

Henry pushes Duggie's head down then takes the manuscript off Berry.

Henry: Concentrate on the sword James.

Berry: ... therefore be a brutal and degraded man — and not so skilful as the hangman — "who is an /artist" (Berry is about to bring the sword down)

Henry: Wait! *(Douglas flinches)* After "degraded". That's where you bring the sword down. Just missing his head mind.

Berry: It'll need a bit of rehearsing.

Douglas stands up, takes off blindfold.

Henry: I'll have him doing it blindfolded before long.

Douglas: What's next?

Berry: Strangulation.

Berry puts down the sword, holds a strap aloft and takes his manuscript off Henry.

Henry: Forthcoming autobiography.

Berry: *(Performing)* "The Spanish method of execution by means of the garrotte has been much praised by some advocates of reform — but death by strangulation is much slower and more painful than death by dislocation. In one form of the garrotting chair … "

Berry breaks off from addressing the audience and addresses Douglas

Would it be possible to construct a chair for strangulation purposes?

Douglas: You can have one from dressing room.

Berry: "In one form of the garrotting chair, this fact has been recognised — an iron spike is placed immediately behind the neck."

Douglas gets hold of chair.

Douglas: Ere, you do it.

Henry now becomes the assistant and sits in the chair. Berry points to where the spike would be, hands the manuscript to

Douglas. Berry is now a more confident presenter of capital punishment.

BERRY: So that when the pressure is applied the spike enters between the two vertebra and severs the spinal cord.

Henry acts dead, tongue protruding.

When the use of electricity for executions began to be talked of as a practical possibility, I naturally took much interest …

DOUGLAS: I can't afford electrocution chair.

BERRY: And so, after careful consideration of all the principle modes of execution, I am convinced that our English method is at present the best yet known.

Berry takes the rope back out of his case.

The most important item is the rope. It must of course be strong. *(Berry pulls the rope)* It must be pliable in order to tighten freely. It should be as thin as possible, but of course not so thin as to rupture the blood vessels of the neck. *(He feels Henry's neck)* This rope I used for no less than sixteen executions. My other rope is now in the possession of Madam Tussaud.

Henry climbs the desk Berry follows.

Having measured the man to be hanged, taken his weight, felt the contours of his neck — and felt his muscles — the hangman who has a job of work on hand, must see that his apparatus is in good working order.

If he omits to see to the oiling of his lever and bolts and also the hinges of the trap door, he may easily bungle the whole thing. Then always at eight a clock, after a hearty breakfast, to fortify me, the Chaplain will reads from the Burial of the Dead.

HENRY: "Now Christ is risen from the dead."

BERRY: The criminal's legs are tied *(Berry ties his legs)*. He looks at the world for one remaining moment — his head and face is covered with the white cap — at last the noose touches his neck — and often in this moment, when the dreadful reality bursts upon him — he faints, half dead with fear. *(Henry pretends to faint, Berry supports him for a moment)* He is supported. *(Then pulls an imaginary lever and Henry drops through the trap door.)* until he has to be supported no more. "Whoso sheddeth man's blood, by man shall his blood be shed."

Berry walks to the front of the stage to take a bow.

DOUGLAS: Supposin' something goes wrong. With apparatus?

Berry turns annoyed that his moment has been ruined

BERRY: Then it will not be the hangman who is to blame.

Scene Two

Two weeks later. Evelyn is in the dressing room facing a mirror, preparing for her turn. Enter Douglas. Douglas is wearing a bow tie. He has a newspaper in his pocket. He stands behind her.

DOUGLAS: There's a table booked.

EVELYN: Is there?

DOUGLAS: Aye. You look lovely. *(He kisses her head)* Been some good houses this week.

EVELYN: I know.

DOUGLAS: Gonna get this place on its feet again.

EVELYN: Are yer?

DOUGLAS: Bank manager was in last night. Impressed him.

EVELYN: Did yer?

DOUGLAS: Aye.

EVELYN: Douglas?

DOUGLAS: What my love?

EVELYN: Can you tell me something?

Douglas: Anything.

Evelyn: Can you tell me, why I found a hangman, in my dressing room?

Douglas: Ah, I meant to tell yer about that. Been busy. I'll tell him to keep out of your way shall I?

Evelyn: If you wouldn't mind. That's not the point though is it?

Douglas: I thought you wouldn't approve.

Evelyn: I don't. In what way, is a hangman, an act?

Douglas: Well, the audience like to hear, about his work. They like his stories. And he's funny.

Evelyn: I didn't laugh when I opened the door to find him tying a noose in the mirror.

Douglas: They laugh in the stalls. And look, he's in the papers.

Takes out a paper from his pocket to show Evelyn

Evelyn: Still doesn't make him an act.

Douglas: We're gonna make him into one.

Evelyn: How?

Douglas: Not sure yet. I was thinking optical projection. Might get a sound effects man in.

Evelyn: You should buy him a song

Douglas: I don't know if he sings.

Evelyn slaps Duggie with the paper.

Evelyn: Christ Duggie!

Pause — one beat

Why can't yer just let the bank have this place eh?

Douglas: No.

Evelyn: Then let Henry have it. What the sly bugger deserves.

Douglas: No. Our life's in here.

Evelyn: We were supposed to be having a life outside.

Douglas: We will.

Evelyn: When you finally get the guts to do it. "Pay off the house, clear the decks on this place … leave Gladys."

Douglas: House is nearly paid for.

Evelyn: Well then. Can't go on like this forever.

Douglas: When I sell this place it has to be doing well.

Evelyn: Never gonna do well. Never has.

Douglas: Not true. Look one or two more new turns, a good season, that's all it'll take.

Evelyn: You're no good as an owner. I stay for you Duggie, for you. When you bought this place as an investment, it was supposed to be a ticket, our ticket. Now we're chained to the walls.

Pause — two beats

Diya know what would be nice? To live by the sea. Wouldn't that be nice eh?

Douglas: What would we do?

Evelyn: We'd be together.

Douglas: Be like starting again.

Evelyn: People do it everyday. 'Cept we can't even get to Whitby for a weekend, cos you're rehearsing an executioner.

Evelyn's turn bell. She's on in one minute. She stands.

Douglas: I'm doin' all this for us yer know.

Evelyn: Are yer?

Douglas: Aye. Do anything for you.

Evelyn: Then get rid of the hangman.

Douglas: What? No.

Evelyn: Yes.

Douglas: I can't. Evelyn, he's just a novelty.

Evelyn: Then he won't be missed will he?

Douglas: Why do I have to?

Evelyn: I help people escape Duggie. Give them something pretty to take home in their hearts. This may not be much of a place but it is music hall. He's not.

Douglas: He's a novelty act and I booked him.

Evelyn: Well I don't want him near me, or you for that matter.

Douglas: He'll make us a few bob, you'll see.

The turn bell rings again. Evelyn exiting.

Evelyn: And that'll be the only thing keeping you warm at night.

A stage curtain comes down and Evelyn performs 'Let The Great Big world keep Turning' (words by Clifford Grey music by Nat D Ayer)

> **Verse**
> If I knew that someone cared for me
> I'd let the world go by
> Someone who was true as true could be
> I'd never want to sigh
> What would I give today?

Just to hear someone softly say

Chorus
Let the great big world keep turning
Never mind if I've got you;
For I only know
That I want you so
And there's no one else will do
You have simply set me yearning,
After ever I'll be true
Let the great big world keep on turning round
Now I've found someone like you

Verse
Love they say must come to one and all
Of high and low degree
Come what may
I'm waiting for the call It holds no fear for me
Maybe the day is near
When the thought of my heart I'll hear

Repeat: chorus

Scene Three

Lights up on the office. It's been more than a week since Evelyn (or Gladys) kept Douglas warm at night. Berry is smoking a cigar.

BERRY: "Aye" I said. "I'm in the habit of giving drops that would cure your tooth ache and your seasickness all in one. But I don't think you'd like me remedy." Then I gave him one of me cards. Should've seen the look on his face.

Berry takes out his hipflask and tops up his own drink.

DOUGLAS: Aye, I can imagine.

HENRY: A toast. To a unique act eh?

They drink.

BERRY: I am sorry about the other night. How is the young lad?

HENRY: He's fine James. Don't you worry about him.

DOUGLAS: You need to be more careful with that sword

BERRY: He moved. I swear/he did.

HENRY: It was his own fault. Anyway, we've had full houses since.

BERRY: Funny but the public seem to appreciate me more than when I was working. Now, when diya think the use of execution was at its height in this country?

HENRY: Do tell us James

BERRY: Now I bet you're thinking, Henry the Eighth, aren't yer?

HENRY: I was about to say that. Any suggestions Douglas … ?

Pause — two beats

BERRY: Edward the Sixth: five hundred and sixty each year at Tyburn alone. Henry only managed two thousand countrywide.

HENRY: Well I never

DOUGLAS: You're a very knowledgeable man Mr Berry.

BERRY: Rather a solemn subject, I know.

HENRY: It's fascinating

DOUGLAS: There are people these days who advocate for the abolition of hanging.

BERRY: There are

HENRY: They don't tend to like music hall though.

BERRY: I've met a number of these people and I always say to them this. Whenever there is a period in which several persons have been found guilty of murder and reprieved, the number of murders increases. However whenever there is a series of executions, the number of murders decreases.

DOUGLAS: Is hanging not murder then?

BERRY: No. It is the carrying out of a divine command.

DOUGLAS: God's work?

HENRY: James has retired. Haven't you? He's now a performer, with an audience. For which we are eternally grateful.

BERRY: There's a very different kind of satisfaction in this line of work. I have wondered whether I shouldn't've been in music hall all along.

HENRY: You're a natural. It's obvious. But I have an idea of how we could improve your act.

BERRY: Do you?

HENRY: Yes

BERRY: How?

HENRY: Well, we could make it more dramatic. More realistic. I think we need to get another performer along side you. And I think we need to give the man you hang something to say. A story to tell.

BERRY: About his murder?

Henry: Have you ever hung an innocent man?

Berry: Never. I always took the trouble to look into each case before I hanged em.

Douglas: There must have been those that protested their innocence

Berry: Plenty.

Douglas: Didn't that worry you?

Berry: Not in the least. Certainly there were those that I would rather not have hanged. Joseph Campbell, he murdered his wife. She was a reckless drinker though. Difficult to know whether he should be more pitied than blamed.

Henry: Well … Have you ever wanted to hang someone but couldn't?

Berry: Haven't we all?

Pause—one beat.

Henry: I was thinking, where someone was reprieved. Or a hanging went wrong say?

Pause—two beats.

Berry: I can think of one terrible experience that occurred. Where an execution didn't go as planned.

Henry fills his glass again.

Henry: Go on

Berry: The drop was too long. The rope too thin. And Robert Goodale's head was severed. A decapitation not a hanging. But the length was dictated to me by Norwich Gaol. Not my fault you understand. Henceforth I always provided my own rope.

Berry finishes his drink in one.

Now if you would excuse me gentlemen. I have an appointment with a newspaper.

Exit Berry.

Henry: What are you doing? "Is hanging murder?" Undermining yer turn.

Douglas: I don't like him.

Henry: Box office doesn't mind him

Douglas: Don't like myself for hiring him.

Henry: "Inspired move" you said.

Douglas: He attracts the wrong kind of audience.

Henry: No such thing. He's more of an act than you think he is.

Douglas: I know music hall Henry

HENRY: Like nobody else and I know some things about him too. I've been making enquiries. He wasn't quite the hangman he says he was.

DOUGLAS: How hard can it be?

HENRY: You heard him. Get the weight wrong and the head comes off. An that wasn't the only time. He was always at it apparently. Liverpool, Norwich, Ireland, one cock up after another. He can't add up see. Cost him his job in the end.

DOUGLAS: I knew it. Knew the man was a bloody fraud.

HENRY: Oh aye. Home Secretary sacked him in the end. They're none too happy about his act neither.

DOUGLAS: Right, settles it. We'll get rid shall we?

HENRY: I'd be inclined to agree Duggie. He's wearing a bit thin int he?

DOUGLAS: Bloody tedious

HENRY: As a one man show that is. But … I've got a plan for a double act

DOUGLAS: With who? The Grim Reaper?

HENRY: Not quite. Just someone who walked in his shadow.

Pause — one beat

John 'Babbecombe' Lee

DOUGLAS: Never heard of him. What's he do?

HENRY: Nothing at the moment. In prison. About twenty years ago though he stood on the gallows and swore that God would not allow him to be hung, said that he had foreseen it all in the dream the night before. When the hangman pulled the lever the trap doors refused to move. So they took him aside then pulled the lever again and the doors opened. But each time they put him back on, they wouldn't budge. Three times they tried to hang him. But he was as calm as you like. Protected by the hand of God, because of his innocence. They sent him to jail. And I'm gonna put him alongside the hangman again — on your stage.

DOUGLAS: Berry?

HENRY: A dramatic reconstruction. Relive that morning. We'll get Lee to talk about the murder

DOUGLAS: I dunno.

HENRY: Why?

DOUGLAS: There's such a thing as taste Henry. A hangman's bad enough, but a murderer?

HENRY: He's innocent. That's the whole point.

DOUGLAS: The other acts. You know how superstitious some of em are.

HENRY: Are they so superstitious that they'd rather not have a hall to dance in? Berry on his own; a novelty. Berry and Lee together? You'll have the bank eating out yer hand.

DOUGLAS: Who did he kill?

HENRY: No one

DOUGLAS: Sure?

HENRY: He was supposed to have knocked off his employer. They decided the butler did it—because there was no one else. But there was suspicions of a break in, and his sister who worked there, she had a fella alright. His lawyer never even turned up for the trial. He was stitched up.

DOUGLAS: How'd do find this out?

HENRY: Newspaper pal. People have been petitioning for his release for years. Word is, they're finally gonna grant it.

DOUGLAS: Will he do it? It's a lot to ask.

HENRY: Oh he'll do it. I've spoken to him. Chance to get his own back. Besides, who's gonna give him a job as a butler?

DOUGLAS: Do you know they used to charge people to look round Bedlam Asylum?

HENRY: Bet they paid n all.

DOUGLAS: Haven't you got any singers eh? Can't you go to London and get me Marie Lloyd? Instead you give me a hangman that can't hang and a murderer that didn't kill anyone.

HENRY: You know 'The Boneless Man' Douggie?

DOUGLAS: What about him?

HENRY: He's not really boneless

DOUGLAS: I know it's rickets but /he is an act.

HENRY: It's not the point. The audience want to believe. You will be staging a miracle. You say you're against hanging. You'll be undoing a miscarriage of justice. And, you could also make a lot of money.

DOUGLAS: Think so?

HENRY: Course. It'll be big news. Lee's already a famous prisoner. I'm gonna make him sommat out here. I'm his representative. Having his story told in a Sunday paper to start with. Then we need to get these two together, in here. Make sure they perform no where else.

DOUGLAS: Supposin' Berry's not keen?

HENRY: He'll want to put the record straight. Besides, we've given him a taste for the limelight now. Right I've a train to catch.

Exit Henry. Blackout.

Scene Four

Two days later. Berry has called in to discuss his act with Douglas. He has his black leather bag with him.

BERRY: I've been thinking bout what Henry said, the other day. He's got a point.

DOUGLAS: You think so?

BERRY: I'm keen to improve my act.

DOUGLAS: Of course

BERRY: I have realised that my vocation as an executioner was in the past. I'm now an entertainer.

DOUGLAS: Good

BERRY: So having considered Henry's advice, I've decided upon

DOUGLAS: A double act?

BERRY: Well you might call it that. It does have reference to a terrible experience during my career.

DOUGLAS: I see

BERRY: I was thinking we might dramatise one of my decapitations.

DOUGLAS: What?

BERRY: Incorporate it into the act. I decapitated two men by hanging. Fortnight apart.

DOUGLAS: How?

BERRY: It's not something I'm easy talking about. I got a little tetchy the other day when Henry raised the matter. A hangman has feelings too yer know.

DOUGLAS: I meant how in the act.

BERRY: Oh.

DOUGLAS: Hell of a turn but it sounds a bit dangerous.

BERRY: I can assure you I don't want to take any more heads off. In fact there's no need. Now, take a look at this, if you will.

Berry takes a very realistic wax work head out of his bag. He places it on the desk and Douglas recoils in horror.

Robert Goodale. The head that came off in Norwich. Poisoned his wife. November ... 1884 I think. Anyway. Realistic don't you think? Called in a favour from Madam Tussauds.

DOUGLAS: Where's the rest of him?

BERRY: They want twenty guineas for a complete Goodale. What do you say?

Douglas picks up the head and puts it to one side facing the audience.

Douglas: Look, you're not going to need no model. Henry has found someone–to perform with you. Not someone you can just hang neither.

Berry: Who?

Douglas: A special guest, we'll call him.

Berry: Well I expect to be consulted. I've joined the Variety Artists Federation now you know. Yes. And I wanted to have a word with you about last night.

Douglas: It won't happen again.

Berry: It's happened a number of times.

Douglas: He's barred.

Berry: A man can be injured by cabbages. And I don't just mean physically.

Douglas: I know. Try not to take it to heart. Of course it could be, that you once worked with an audience member's family.

Berry: No reason to throw vegetables at me.

Douglas: Mighta been aimed at the orchestra. Wouldn't be the first time. You're very popular James.

Enter Henry with John Lee walking behind him. John Lee has been in prison for twenty two years. He is man who has been through a living death and is broken in spirit. Berry does not see them but Douglas does, realises who it is and is immediately nervous.

Berry: Did I tell you, I think I've found a publisher — for my autobiography?

Douglas: That's excellent news. What's it called?

Berry: Memories of an Executioner

Douglas: Henry! I wasn't expecting you.

Berry peers over his shoulder and sees Henry and Lee. He doesn't recognise Lee at all.

Berry: Henry I was just telling Douglas here about some plans I ave for the act

Henry: Really?

Berry: Aye.

Berry takes the waxwork head out of the bag and tosses it to Henry

What do you think? I couldn't afford the rest of him.

Henry: An old acquaintance?

Berry: Very jovial man he was.

Henry returns the head to Berry and is confident that the two men do not recognise each other. He risks an introduction.

HENRY: This is my latest turn.

BERRY: Pleased to meet you. What kind of act have yer?

DOUGLAS: We're not sure yet.

BERRY: My act's a novelty. Intrigues people.

DOUGLAS: Look why don't you wait outside James. While I find out exactly, what this gentleman does.

Puts head in case and exits. He sits outside but on stage. Douglas's blood pressure comes down.

Take a seat. Please.

Lee sits. Henry stares at him in deep curiosity. Lee surveys his surroundings. Douglas is pouring whisky for himself.

Would you like a drink?

JOHN: No thank you.

But Douglas needs one.

DOUGLAS: I'm Douglas. The owner. John, did Henry explain to you why you are here?

John: He came to see me in Portland Jail. He said that if I came to you, you would pay me, to tell folk what happened to me on the gallows.

Douglas: That's right. Only you will have to do a little more than 'tell folk'. Did you used to go to the music hall?

John: No

Douglas: Never?

John: Never sir.

Pause — two beats

Douglas: Do you know what one is?

John: Well I have heard of em.

Douglas: This is a music hall. Look there are nine turns. First act always a funny man. Some cockney usually. Then some slip of a girl cutting her teeth. And you move through the bill, acrobats, fat ladies to we get to the big turn. Now of course the nearer the top the more you're paid. That man you've just met — well he's the novelty, that's about half way. After the interval.

John: Is he a funny man?

Douglas: No. Now always before the final act — there's another novelty — 'The Human Fly' or whatever. And we were thinking of putting you — and that gentleman on before the last turn. To talk about hanging.

John: Why will I be with that man?

Douglas: Didn't he /explain to you … ?

Henry: I thought I'd give him time. / To adjust.

Douglas: Christ Henry. You don't recognise him then?

John: No sir.

Henry: Mr Berry hasn't always been an entertainer.

John: What does he do?

Douglas: He entertains audiences by …

Henry: … by telling them about all the people he has hung.

Douglas: Except for one.

Pause — one beat.

Henry: That one being you.

There is silence. John Lee gets up and walks about the office. This moment could crush him — he is frightened but interested.

John: Does he still hang people?

Henry: No John.

John: And it was him that tried to hang me?

Pause — two beats

HENRY: We want you to stand upon the gallows and tell everyone what it felt like twenty years ago. About to be hung, knowing you were innocent, saved by almighty God.

DOUGLAS: Is it true you dreamt that they wouldn't be able to hang you?

JOHN: It is.

HENRY: Then tell everyone. Tell them about the murder and the trial

DOUGLAS: tell them that you were innocent

HENRY: and we will recreate the hanging.

DOUGLAS: We can help you with the lines

HENRY: I know a writer

JOHN: No harm will come to me?

DOUGLAS: You'll be famous.

Pause — one beat.

JOHN: No writer would be able to do it.

HENRY: Can you do it John?

DOUGLAS: How well do you remember?

JOHN: How well? I am always conscious of all that passed. Just as I was on the morning.

DOUGLAS: Go on

Pause — one beat.

JOHN: I wake at half six. I am calm. I wait. When I hear the prison bell start to boom I know it is time. Berry comes with the warders, and the chaplain. He holds out his hand, so I shake it. Before I knew where I am, he slips a belt round my waist, buckles it and straps my arms to it. Then he leads me out and we walk, like a procession following a coffin, to the coach house across a garden. The doors are flung wide apart and I can see a rope. I wonder how I will be dropped down though. A trap never occurs to me see. I reckon I'm to be pushed off a height into space. Then Berry puts a bag over my head. Like a pillow-case, except that it has elastic where it fits round the neck. Then I feel something being placed around my neck. The rope. For the moment I am conscious of a strange sensation in my throat. My mouth goes dry. I can feel the executioner's fingers about my neck. I feel him pull the rope, til it pinches me under the left ear. I hold my breath and clench my teeth. I hear the chaplain's voice. I hear the clang of the bell. I hear a wrench as of a bolt drawn, and then — what is this? Death? Some nightmare? The trap has dropped about two inches. A second passes. And it is like a lifetime. They are stamping on the boards. I stand on the drop blind-folded and strapped whilst the warders jump on the boards to make them part. I am resting on my toes, and every time the warders stamp, the trap shakes. Again and again the bolt is drawn, but the mechanism will not work. For something like six minutes I hover there. That would've been enough to kill a man I suppose, but I stand quiet. Then they take me off the trap. The cap, rope and leg straps are taken off, and I am taken into a little store room about six yards from the shed. Whilst I am there I think an officer hangs on to the rope, and is dropped through the trap, so I know, they have it working now.

Douglas: How long are you waiting?

John: I am in that room for something like four minutes. I can hear them pulling the bolt backwards and forwards. Each time there is a thud as the trap is released and falls inwards. Then Berry comes for me again. He takes me back to the shed where the officials are waiting. Some of them turn away. They can't look at me. The warders are white as ghosts. Once more my legs are strapped and once more the cap and rope are adjusted. When the drop gives I feel my fall into space begin. The shock takes away my breath. I want to put out my hands and grasp something. It seems as if my heart is leaping out of my body. Death, does not come. I sink two inches just as before. And the bell is still tolling. What is passing in my mind all this time I don't really know. Each time the bolt is drawn I think I am gone. For the moment I experience a strange sensation like that falling sinking feeling you get in a nightmare. It continues each time until consciousness returns and I feel my feet still on the boards.

Douglas: What do you remember about Berry?

John: He's cursing and stamping on doors because they won't open. He pulls me aside like an animal. He keeps shouting "Drop yer bugger".

HENRY: I don't imagine it was personal

Pause — one beat

JOHN: What does he say about me — the hangman?

HENRY: He admires you John. Everyone does.

DOUGLAS: You think you could tell an audience?

JOHN: When they told me they had given up, I rejoiced. *(Pause)* That was because I didn't know I had been saved from one tomb to be sent to another. *(Pause)* Prisoners aren't allowed much conversation. I've hardly spoke about it til now. If he is being paid for his story then I want to be paid more than him. Double.

Henry immediately walks over to John and shakes his hand.

HENRY: Done. Now John, I want you to write down what you've told us and bring it to me. I suppose you got a bit of catching up to do, so we'll see you in a few days for a rehearsal. Douglas my client will need an advance for board and lodgings. *(Douglas Hands over twenty pounds) (Escorting John out)* Now, I can understand that you may feel a little resentful towards Mr Berry, personally I don't blame you. Not for a minute. But try not to let it stand in the way. Think of him as someone who can help you tell your story.

On exit Lee walks past Berry outside the office. He stops and looks at him for a moment. Henry follows but stands a little distance away.

BERRY: Oh any luck sir?

JOHN: I don't think it was luck.

John holds out his hand to shake Berry's.

BERRY: Perhaps we'll meet back stage.

Pause — one beat.

JOHN: Aye we might.

Exit Lee.

HENRY: What do you think?

DOUGLAS: It's an interesting story I'll give you that, but it does make yer feel a bit ... gloomy, dunt it?

HENRY: We'll make it theatrical. More exciting.

DOUGLAS: Aren't we just inviting the audience to a hanging here?

HENRY: Used to get good crowds.

Henry beckons Berry

James.

Berry enters office

Take a seat. Do you remember the case of John Lee? I'm sure you do. It was in the papers at the time. The butler who tried to hack off his ladyship's head.

BERRY: It was a dreadful case. I don't like to think about it. Even now.

HENRY: No. Sounds awful.

BERRY: Aye, it was. Mechanism failed and the bugger escaped me. Ruined me career.

HENRY: We understand.

BERRY: They didn't at the time. They blamed me. Blamed God even.

DOUGLAS: What do you think happened?

BERRY: The gallows had been placed outside in a yard. I should have realised then. The ironwork on them was too frail, the trap doors were only one board deep. Too weak for the purpose. And it had rained solidly for two days.

HENRY: How well do you remember that morning?

BERRY: Like yesterday.

Pause — one beat. Berry drifts into his recollection.

Eight o'clock on Monday, February twenty third, 1885, was the time fixed for his execution. At the appointed time, I bring out the prisoner in the usual way. He says nothing to me. Seems unaffected. I think it's to be straight forward. I pinion him, draw my white cap over his head, then tighten the noose. I wait for the chaplain to finish, stand back and pull the lever. I hear the noise of the bolts sliding apart–but the doors do not fall. He's still stood there, in front of me, between life and death. I stamp on the drop to shake it loose. The warders are jumping that hard they're gonna go into pit with him, but none of our efforts can stir it. When we take him off, I pull the lever and the doors open. I keep trying, but they won't open for him. The chaplain faints and Lee is taken back to his cell.

HENRY: And gets life

BERRY: Then all the talk began about his innocence and providence but it was nothing.

DOUGLAS: What was it?

BERRY: The rain. Soaked the untreated wood. When he stood on the boards they expanded and jammed. That's all. It was a convict carpenter that built his gallows.

DOUGLAS: An he set it up to fail?

BERRY: He says that now. He were a bodger. Either way, John Lee should be in hell.

HENRY: He's a free man. They've released him.

BERRY: I would make it illegal to petition. He attracted sentiment because … of a cock up. That's all.

Douglas: You don't think he was innocent?

Berry: Evidence was overwhelming

Henry: I here somebody got to his lawyer.

Berry: By all accounts his legal representative was not a moral man.

Henry: And there were no witnesses and no confession.

Berry: I followed the case. Read the depositions. She was murdered near where he slept. The cleaver was from a drawer in the pantry, where he slept. The body was set alight and the oil found on his clothes.

Henry: From putting out the fire, he said at the trial.

Berry: What about the blood?

Henry: He cut his arm, breaking a window to let the smoke out.

Berry: He was the only man in the house, and only a man could have inflicted such wounds. The skull was smashed in and the head nearly cut off. And only a man would have had the strength to move the body.

Henry: Maybe some one else, another man, got in the house. I heard the cook did a bit of entertaining herself.

Berry: Certainly, she was expecting, at the time of the trial. But Lee's bed was in the pantry, off the kitchen, not far from hers. True the kitchen door was open, but any intruder would have to ave crept past him and her. And taken the hatchet and the oil from the drawer. Emma Keyse was hacked death a few yards from his bed. It's inconceivable that Lee would have slept through it. It was him.

HENRY: But he had no reason to kill her.

Pause — two beats.

BERRY: He knows why he did it.

DOUGLAS: He says he dreamt the night before that he wouldn't be hung.

BERRY: So have plenty of others. If God spared Lee it wasn't so that he could play innocent. Look, it was a stain on my career. Some hangmen rallied round. Others pointed the finger, stabbed me in the back. They were after the work. Bugger finished me in the end.

HENRY: He's sold his story to a newspaper.

BERRY: I don't doubt it. People will pay for any sensationalist rubbish these days

DOUGLAS: But he's also interested in telling his story, at music halls

BERRY: Not much of a story

HENRY: It's an incredible story.

Pause as Berry begins to realise where this is going

Let him tell it alongside you.

BERRY: Why? Never!

HENRY: Because you will be able to show what really happened. Re-enact it on the gallows. It wasn't his innocence, it wasn't God, it wasn't your fault, it was just — the rain.

DOUGLAS: A chance to put the record straight.

HENRY: If we don't, he'll be off down City Varieties.

DOUGLAS: Of course you'll have to show him the ropes.

HENRY: You're a performer

DOUGLAS: You know the business

HENRY: You're in charge of the act.

DOUGLAS: Unofficially.

HENRY: Just as you were on the day. Once the public have seen him with you, he won't be able to perform alone.

Pause. Berry opens his case and takes out a rope with a noose. He stares at it.

BERRY: I never employed it after that morning. But I've kept it these past twenty years. I'm told it would fetch a few pounds at auction.

Henry touches the rope.

Interesting to see him wear it again. You know I've always thought that execution was a kind of performance. One can imagine the pressure of a public event.

DOUGLAS: Indeed

BERRY: This isn't going to be easy for me. Painful memories. I expect an increase in my fee.

HENRY: Naturally. Details James. In principle you agree?

BERRY: In principle he should be hanged. I look forward to meeting him.

Exit Berry assuredly.

HENRY: What's wrong?

DOUGLAS: Suppossin' Lee is guilty?

HENRY: Who cares?

DOUGLAS: I do. You heard him. They only started believing he was innocent because they couldn't/hang him

HENRY: No no. Look, he claimed his innocence from the beginning. Right until he had the rope round his neck. Besides, it's what audience believes that matters. Just one thing missing now.

Scene Four

Evelyn enters in performance costume. Douglas plays the piano and she sings first verse and chorus of 'Let Me Call You Sweetheart'. Whilst Evelyn is singing the manager's office is struck and a gallows is wheeled on.

Scene Five

The noose of the gallows casts a shadow onto the back wall as it gently swings. Enter John. He stares at the gallows. John surveys the gallows and hesitates to touch the construction. Enter Evelyn behind John.

EVELYN: It's a strange thing, to see. In a music hall.

JOHN: I didn't expect to see one again.

EVELYN: No. You should be spared this.

JOHN: Henry says it what folks want to see these days. My experience is what they want to hear about.

EVELYN: Henry is a vulgar man.

JOHN: The public are interested.

EVELYN: If you were actors, it would be different then. It would be an act.

JOHN: It cannot be acted. It has to be me. I am John 'Babbecombe' Lee, 'The Man They Couldn't Hang'.

EVELYN: You better hope so.

Pause — one beat.

JOHN: I'm assured no harm will come to me.

Evelyn: No. You're going to be famous up there.

John: Certainly has been a lot of commotion about me. Henry's arranged for me to have signed photographs to sell. In the Sunday papers as well. I'm writing everything down. People can easily get all at sea with the facts.

Evelyn: Is it a fact you dreamt you wouldn't be hanged?

John: I saw the route to the scaffold in my dream. Although I'd never walked it before. An that night a candlestick fell off the table at my mother's. But although the candle broke in two, the light refused to go out.

Evelyn: A miracle then?

John: I dunno. I do know on the Sunday before the execution, I was prayed for in all the Exeter Churches. Not everything they say about me is true. It's not true that two white doves flew about the scaffold. Not true that I made threats against certain officers.

Evelyn: How long were you in prison for John?

John: Twenty two years. Kept me longer than they had a right to. I've seen your name outside. Big letters.

Evelyn: Have you ever seen the music hall?

John: I was thinking bout coming in, tonight.

Evelyn: You should.

JOHN: My mother had a fine voice. Lizzie too. *(Pause)* At my age most men have a knowledge of the world. I feel like a child sometimes.

EVELYN: Then the music hall will suit you John. Why put yourself through this though, the gallows again, every night?

JOHN: Prove my innocence. I'll be famous.

EVELYN: You will. Men will be in awe of you, and some women excited I expect.

JOHN: I hope so.

EVELYN: Music hall is full of women, and men with ideas about them. Suppose you've got a bit of catching up to do.

Enter Douglas.

DOUGLAS: All set eh? First rehearsal. Exciting int it?

EVELYN: I hear you got the decorators coming in.

DOUGLAS: Place could do with a coat.

EVELYN: An I bet it costs.

DOUGLAS: Bank manager approves.

EVELYN: Likes the hangman does he?

Douglas: He can see the attraction. Have you been introduced? John this is Miss Evelyn Nesbitt, she's a female vocalist.

John: I'm comin' to watch her tonight.

Douglas: Where's the hell's Berry. *(Looking to John for confirmation)* He's not usually late is he?

John: What do you want me to wear Mr Fawcett?

Douglas: For the performance?

John: My prison suit is rather beggarly.

Douglas: Then wear it. And don't be afraid to let people in the street know who you are. And who's music hall you're at.

Evelyn: For tonight though, it might be better if Douglas buys you a new suit.

Douglas: Look, shouldn't you be restin' yer voice?

Evelyn: I shall look out for you John.

Exit Evelyn. Enter Berry. This is the first time that these two have met since the botched hanging twenty two years ago.

Douglas: Mr Berry. Right, now. You two know each other of course. Obviously it was a while ago. Bygones be bygones n all that. So, how shall we start this? A dramatic opening. John.

Douglas fetches a chair from off stage

You're in the cell. So, you need to be doomed faced.

John sits, his demeanour doesn't change

Aye that's perfect. Mr Berry, on the gallows if you please.

Berry climbs them.

You need to look … no don't act. And this is where the lights will come up, like dawn. Some dramatic music. The light will be on Mr Lee at first, Mr Berry more in shadow. Then …

BERRY: My Experiences as an Executioner!

DOUGLAS: Ah, we've a different title now. 'The Man They Couldn't Hang!'

BERRY: I'm not saying that. Not strictly true.

DOUGLAS: Up til now it has been. Look, it's a double act.

BERRY: I am aware of that, but not at my expense it's not.

DOUGLAS: You'll get to say why he wasn't hanged. Now I want you both to say it.

BERRY: We could call it, 'Under Sentence /of Death'

DOUGLAS: No! Alright I'll introduce. Then we must go back …

JOHN: Go to the trial next.

DOUGLAS: No we go … to the kitchen.

BERRY: Can I make a suggestion?

DOUGLAS: What?

BERRY: The Executioner at Home. I'm scanning the newspapers. I see there is a case in Devon. I mark it, no, I read /out from the paper

DOUGLAS: It's not set up for domestic.

BERRY: Shouldn't take long

DOUGLAS: We haven't time. I've enough overheads with all that.

BERRY: Hardly well made

DOUGLAS: Not meant to work. Whole bloody point. Remember twenty minutes. S'all you've got.

JOHN: Took longer on the day

DOUGLAS: We will start—with the night of murder.

BERRY: At long last.

DOUGLAS: Now, John. It has occurred to me that you ought to be dressed as a butler. You haven't still got the uniform have yer?

JOHN: No

DOUGLAS: Can you talk about the life of a servant?

JOHN: Aye

DOUGLAS: How miserable it was. Was it miserable?

JOHN: At times certainly.

DOUGLAS: Smashing

JOHN: I lived in a space no bigger than a cupboard.

DOUGLAS: Wonderful.

JOHN: And for no more than two shillings a week.

DOUGLAS: Perfect

JOHN: Less than a man /could live on.

DOUGLAS: Aye alright. We've got the picture!

BERRY: Are we gonna talk about Miss Keyse at all?

DOUGLAS: In a moment. What do you remember. About the night of the murder?

JOHN: I was woken by the smell of burning. So I rushed out of the pantry and saw that the house was full of smoke. I woke everyone I could. Lizzie and the others. Lizzie went into missus room but she couldn't find her. We found her in the drawing room. It was her that was on fire.

DOUGLAS: The murderer set fire to her?

JOHN: Aye

DOUGLAS: I like that. Nice touch that.

JOHN: I broke a window to let the smoke out. That's how I cut my arm yer see.

DOUGLAS: Right.

JOHN: Then I went to the village to get help. When I came back they arrested me on suspicion of murder. I wasn't worried though.

DOUGLAS: You have to say that.

JOHN: I knew God would protect me

DOUGLAS: Of course

BERRY: Didn't protect you at the trial.

JOHN: There were no witnesses

BERRY: Save your own sister

JOHN: She's was my half sister and she saw nothing

DOUGLAS: Could you say she was your sister — for the act?

John: No.

Douglas: All right so, before the execution …

John: I dreamt I wouldn't be hung.

Douglas: I want you to describe the dream.

John takes some notes out of his pocket to consult.

James, can you remember that night?

Berry: I can. I was restless.

Douglas: Naturally–you had to hang someone …

Berry: No it were the apparatus. I knew it weren't right.

Douglas: But you dreamt?

Berry: I can't rightly remember

Douglas: You must have dreamt.

Berry: Possibly

Douglas: Just tell the audience you bloody dreamt man! That John Lee would not be hanged. That's all you need to say.

Berry: I think it is time the executioner prepared.

Douglas: High time Mr Berry

Berry climbs the gallows. Takes the existing rope off and takes original rope out of briefcase, fixes it to the scaffold.

BERRY: I examine the trap doors. I notice how flimsy they are. One board thick. The wood is untreated, the apparatus has been left out in the rain

DOUGLAS: There was a storm. More Biblical.

Enter Henry. He has several newspapers under his arm. Henry observes from a distance

BERRY: I thought this was to be a reconstruction. You said it was a reconstruction.

DOUGLAS: It is. You have a gallows, the rope and someone you once tried to hang.

BERRY: A dream is one thing sir, but I don't agree with God being brought into this.

DOUGLAS: He's in every night.

BERRY: It wasn't God in Exeter. It was the rain

JOHN: And who makes it rain?

BERRY: It was February.

JOHN: *(John gets up angry)* Three times you tried to hang me. I never seen a man so angry as you that morning

BERRY: I had a job to do.

John: Why is it that you enjoy it so much then?

Berry: There are worse ways to die John Lee

John ascends gallows to square up to Berry

Douglas: Flaming Nora!

John: Plenty knew my innocence. Reckon you would have been happier hanging an innocent man.

Berry: You charlatan!

Douglas sits on the chair despairing.

Henry: Innocent, guilty, what does it matter? John Lee is the man who cheated death. People are paying to be entertained, hang the truth, audiences pay, juries don't. Gentlemen, your photographs are in the music hall press, your names are all over the papers.

He holds up the papers, they descend to have a look. Berry looks at papers avidly.

You're no longer like other ordinary people. Ordinary people will pay to see you, so make sure you don't disappoint them. I've been speaking to a music hall manager in Manchester. He wants you over there. He'll pay well. So, do you think you can stand on the gallows together again, or not?

John: One thing I been meaning to ask you Henry

HENRY: Go on

JOHN: If the trap doors are going to open when I stand off them — how do I know they're gonna stay shut, when I stand on em?

HENRY: It's a music hall secret that is. Don't worry you're much too valuable to hang John. So ... look why don't you two gentlemen go to the pub over the road and have a drink together? Get acquainted in different environment. Might help matters mightn't it?

BERRY: What do you say John Lee?

JOHN: I'd say my throat feels dry.

John exits followed by Berry.

DOUGLAS: What diyer mean Manchester?

HENRY: I was whetting their appetite. That's all.

DOUGLAS: I don't trust you

HENRY: You know what you need? Exclusivity clauses. Stop your artists performing anywhere else.

DOUGLAS: Acts I have generally don't.

HENRY: They soon will. I had a word with me newspaper pal.

Hands Douglas a copy of Variety.

Mind you his editor in't so keen

Douglas: What's he say? (Turning the pages)

Henry: "Affront to public decency". No look it gets better. You're in the Telegraph. They want to know if this is what Lee was released from jail for? Member of Parliament wants the act banned. Marvellous.

Douglas: I'll loose me license.

Henry: You'll loose this place if you don't get the punters. When will the decorators be finished?

Douglas: Another week.

Henry: Did you get a price from the builders?

Douglas: Yeah n I nearly put that rope around me neck. And I'm having trouble with the gallows.

Henry: How diya mean?

Douglas: It's complicated. Mechanism's a specialist job, sometimes it seems to work alright then …

Henry: What?

Douglas: The trap doors keep opening when they shouldn't.

Henry: No good that. Need to get it right Duggie.

Douglas: Wrong's what we need to get it.

Scene Six

A pub, indicated mostly by light and sound. John sits downstage and Berry approaches from behind carrying two drinks. We hear a pub piano playing a few bars of 'Let Me Call You Sweetheart'.

BERRY: I think our act together looks promising. I think they will like it.

JOHN: I don't know.

BERRY: They will. How are you adjusting to freedom John Lee?

JOHN: Everybody and everything is in a hurry. Whilst in prison I read everything they'd let me, so I knew what would be waiting for me outside.

BERRY: A lot of changes to get used to.

JOHN: The world flies round in a whirlwind.

BERRY: You will adjust in time.

JOHN: Prison strips a man of independence. Either makes him helpless or makes him worse.

BERRY: You must try and be hopeful John. There must be things you want to do?

JOHN: I dunno. I miss my mother. Barely been home since I was released. Babbecombe seemed very much as it was.

Though my old school friends are now mothers and fathers with families of their own.

BERRY: There is time for you to have a family.

JOHN: I'd like to. What about you, have any family. A wife and child?

BERRY: My wife died. A long time ago it was. The children grown up now

JOHN: Do they visit you?

BERRY: We had difficult times in the past. Wasn't an easy life as a hangman you know. I don't expect you to care.

JOHN: Go on.

BERRY: I was forced to move house by people. The children were punished for what I did.

JOHN: You think of taking another job then?

BERRY: No I didn't. Your half sister, the cook … ?

JOHN: Lizzie. Died in the workhouse.

BERRY: Oh. You were close back then.

JOHN: Well we didn't write. Not after the trial.

BERRY: It wasn't her evidence alone John. As I remember there was a stack a people pointing the finger at you. You have an opportunity here John. You've not been out in the world much. This business we're in, it's cutthroat, believe me. Henry and Douglas aim to make money from us.

JOHN: I know

BERRY: We have to make sure we are paid fairly. Both of us. Now I have joined the Variety Artists Federation.

He takes out a card to show John

JOHN: What's that?

BERRY: A trade union. For musical hall performers.

JOHN: Why?

BERRY: Well. You see I asked for a raise, in my turn fee, for the double act. To seven pound a turn. And I think you deserve to be paid the same.

Pause

Are they paying you the same?

JOHN: No. I'm paid different to you.

BERRY: You see. You should contact the union and they would insist you were paid the same as me.

JOHN: I'll think about it. All seems an odd way for people to be entertained.

BERRY: We should bear in mind what Henry is saying. What happened in the past is not important now.

JOHN: What happened in the past is all I am. There's more to all this than Henry explained to me.

BERRY: What is it about the act that's bothering you?

John looks askance.

JOHN: Like I keep having to relive that night, and that morning. Relive my death. And I don't like the way things are being dragged up.

BERRY: Merely a show.

JOHN: Maybe I'll go back to Babbecombe, think about all this

BERRY: There isn't time. We must perform next week.

JOHN: I dunno.

John finishes his drink, stands about to leave.

I know what my mother would say about this, she'd say I was being made a scapegoat, all over again.

BERRY: You have signed a contract.

JOHN: Can't send me back to prison for it.

BERRY: No. John. Wait. John. Please! Sit down. You don't know music hall do you? It isn't only the music. People pay to see things. Tremendous things. The Elephant Man, The Blood Drinker. Our presence together is a tremendous thing.

JOHN: You think so?

BERRY: Yes. There was a crowd for you at Torquay wasn't there? The men at the bar know who you are. People in the street will come up to you. Take you by the hand. Thousands of people will see us John.

JOHN: You don't still wish you'd hung me?

BERRY: Not now no.

JOHN: Because I can be part of your act.

BERRY: I believed in your guilt, the morning I tried to hang you. A hangman has to. How else can he take the job?

JOHN: What do you think now?

BERRY: I think you should proclaim your innocence on stage. What matters now John is the show. More than anything; people must believe in the show.

A few bars of Let Me Call You Sweetheart, fade to black.

Interval

Act II

Scene Seven

A week later. Mid morning. John is sitting upon the gallows listening to Evelyn sing, 'I Was a Good Little Girl Till I Met You' (Clifford Harris and James W Tate). Evelyn sings out to the audience.

>When I was young and innocent
>You stole into my heart
>You taught me things I now repent
>Whenever we're apart
>You taught me that the world was wide
>A bit too wide for me
>And now I am not satisfied with just a cup of tea
>I was a good little girl till I met you
>You sent my head in a whirl
>My poor heart too
>Oh how you told me the tale
>You always do

Evelyn suddenly stops; hesitates.

JOHN: Go on.

EVELYN: I don't think I'll sing it.

JOHN: Why?

EVELYN: Douglas doesn't like it.

JOHN: I like it.

EVELYN: Do you?

JOHN: I do. Makes me smile.

EVELYN: Well maybe I will then.

Pause — one beat

JOHN: Is he your chap, Douglas?

EVELYN: Thinks he is.

JOHN: Not properly then?

EVELYN: Did you have a sweetheart. Before?

JOHN: For a while.

EVELYN: What was she like?

JOHN: Kind, pretty. A sought after woman she was.

EVELYN: You would have married her?

JOHN: No. Couldn't. We had to keep it secret. Another servant she was. And people didn't approve of that.

EVELYN: But if you'd've been married.

JOHN: We didn't talk about it. Just a dalliance to begin with. I used to sneak into her kitchen when Miss Keyse was out. But then we were together more and more. Til I was taken for the killing of Miss Keyse.

Evelyn: Do you know what happened to her?

John: Died in the workhouse. Must be exciting, to be a performer.

Evelyn: It was.

John: Douglas said you were very famous.

Evelyn: No. Is this all you want to do John. The music hall?

John: It's a position of a sort. Not much else I can do.

Evelyn: You can still have another life.

John: I've no trade. I won't be a servant again.

Evelyn: What would you have liked to have been?

John: A sailor. I was a sailor once. When I was nineteen. I sailed all over. Good seaman I was.

Evelyn: What happened?

John: Caught pneumonia. Invalided out. *(Pause)* Maybe I'll sail again.

Evelyn: Less than a fortnight to America now.

John: But I have a chance to clear my name here.

Evelyn: You feel you must do that?

John: I didn't kill Emma Keyse.

Pause — one beat.

Evelyn: I know.

Pause — one beat.

John: Are you a member of this Federation?

Evelyn: The union. Aye, I am.

John: Mr Berry the hangman has asked me to join.

Evelyn: He's a socialist hangman is he?

John: He says it will make my position strong.

Evelyn: He wants you to join because he's in a weaker position than you now.

Enter Douglas. He unrolls some posters.

Douglas: What do you think? You must be proud.

John: Do you think many people will come then?

Douglas: Of course. Full houses. Gonna do well this place, like it used to. Good start for you this.

Evelyn: John and I were just talking about the Variety Artists Federation.

John: Mr Berry is already a member.

Douglas: I know.

Evelyn: Think about what I said John.

John: I shall be watching you tonight.

Evelyn: I'll be looking out for you.

John is preoccupied with Evelyn as she exits.

Douglas: You don't want to pay too much attention to Evelyn. She can be very moody. *(Pause)* You're not worried are yer son?

John: It will be more difficult than I thought.

Douglas: I know. Look, you can trust the gallows.

John: Mr Berry told me.

Douglas: You don't want to listen to him, blimey. Couldn't hang a pair of curtains that man. Is it him that's bothering you? Because if it is …

John: No. He will not want to hang me now. Now that we are an act together.

Douglas: You trust me don't you kid?

John: I think so

Douglas: If one man has nerves of steel in England John, it's you. Stood on them gallows like a statue didn't you? Do it again. That's the story.

John: I was already dead by then. You die before they hang you.

Douglas: Aye

John: In the slow weeks waiting/for execution.

Douglas: Might be better if don't say that. Sounds a bit morbid.

John: It is true.

Douglas: Not entertaining though. Look if you're wondering, I can't pay you anymore. I've had to shell out a bit recently. You'll be earning more soon.

John: I'm not sure why people are interested.

Douglas: You're a hero John. Your life's been the performance.

John: There is more to my life.

Douglas: Well. I wouldn't feel guilty neither. They sent you to jail for twenty years didn't they? The crowd will love you.

John: I hope so.

Douglas: Oh they will. I know about crowds. You don't know music hall do you? All the years in jail, you don't know what you missed. I did turns once you know. Oh aye, funny man. Jokes, songs. I had laughter cascading over the stalls like waves at Scarborough. Ere this bloke stopped me the other day and said to me, 'Do you know the way to Bury St Edmunds?' Do you know what I said to him?

JOHN: No

DOUGLAS: 'Dig a flaming big hole' I said. 'Do you know we used to have two windmills on our farm, but we had to take one down. Do you know why?'

JOHN: No

DOUGLAS: 'We didn't have enough wind for two.'

Pause — one beat.

JOHN: You don't do it no more then?

DOUGLAS: No. They can break your heart an audience. Like flaming kids they are. Let em down once and they won't trust you. But you won't have to worry about that. You've a straightforward act. You and the hangman. What can go wrong?

Pause — one beat.

JOHN: I dunno.

DOUGLAS: You've got a future here John. Part of a tradition, Variety. People I've had on this stage. A man died out there once. I mean literally died. This Chinaman. Used to stop a bullet with a plate. One night, he just decided not to.

Audience thought it was his act. Best round of applause he ever had. But don't you worry. Nothing's gonna happen to you.

Exit Douglas. He has left the posters. John looks at them. He looks once again at the gallows. He climbs them. We hear a few bars of 'Let Me Call You Sweetheart'

JOHN: They play with our lives I think.

Scene Eight

The next day and the day of the first performance. Douglas is tying a banner to the front of the gallows, 'The Man They Couldn't Hang'. Enter Evelyn.

DOUGLAS: You're early.

EVELYN: I've come to see you.

DOUGLAS: Have yer? What do you think? (The banner)

EVELYN: Very nice Douglas. I've been thinking. About the act. My act. I'd like a change.

DOUGLAS: How'd diya mean?

EVELYN: I want a pianist beside me. The whole time.

DOUGLAS: You've got the whole orchestra.

EVELYN: There's a reason why those four play in a pit. I've decided. I want a piano.

DOUGLAS: Why?

EVELYN: A piano is more dignified. More personal. Not too much to ask is it. To have a gentlemen beside me every night?

DOUGLAS: No. Not sure it's necessary.

EVELYN: But it is necessary to have a murderer and a hangman on stage?

DOUGLAS: John never murdered no one.

EVELYN: Easily taken in you.

DOUGLAS: Berry told me and Henry. The cook were pregnant and she pointed the finger at her own brother to protect the father.

Pause — two beats.

EVELYN: The cook you say?

DOUGLAS: Aye, Lizzie Harris the cook. Her fella must have put the hatchet into her ladyship and done a bunk. Evelyn this won't be for long. I'm trying to get meself into a position where I can walk away, with you.

EVELYN: You've got yerself into more debt is what you've done. And you've no idea what kind of act you've just taken on.

Pause — one beat.

EVELYN: This'll be me last season. With or without you.

DOUGLAS: Don't talk daft.

EVELYN: I've had enough. Too old.

DOUGLAS: Course yer not.

Evelyn: I am. N' I'm tired. The odd Sunday on Scarborough pier'll do me.

Douglas: You're my star turn.

Douglas puts his hands upon her; she doesn't want him to touch her.

Evelyn: I can't do this anymore.

Douglas: I'll play for you. Let me play.

Goes to the piano, begins to play. Plays chorus of 'My Girl's a Yorkshire Girl (E by Gum she's a Champion)'

> My girl's a Yorkshire girl, Yorkshire through and through
> My girl a Yorkshire girl, Eh by gum she's a champion
> Though she's a factory lass, and wears no fancy clothes
> I've a sort of Yorkshire relish for my little Yorkshire Rose

Spoken under the piano music

Douglas: Quaver

Pause — two beats.

Evelyn: Yes... Crotchet

Douglas: Did I tell you someone asked to buy our piano the other day?

Evelyn: No you didn't.

Douglas: He said, "Is it second hand?" I said "yes." He said "I'll give you fifty pound less ten per cent then".

Pause — one beat

Evelyn: What did you say Crotchet?

Douglas: Well Quaver I couldn't work it out. If someone offered you fifty pound less ten per cent, what would you take off?

Evelyn: Everything but me earrings!

Evelyn's sad reluctance abates.

Ere! This officer stopped me the other day

Douglas: What did he say?

Evelyn: He just said "Do yer — or dunt yer?"

Douglas: What did you say?

Evelyn: "You talked me into it."

Douglas: What do you think of my execution on the piano?

Evelyn: I'm in favour of it.

End flourish on the piano.

Douglas: We should've stayed a double act.

Evelyn: Aye we should.

Douglas: You never wanted that. Always wanted the spotlight you.

Evelyn: You shoulda stayed a turn.

Douglas: I'm doin alright. Evelyn, you're not gonna walk out on me are yer? The only act left for me.

Evelyn: Building's all that matters to you.

Douglas: Because you're in it, every night. Think it would mean anything to me if you weren't here?

She kisses him. As they kiss Berry enters behind Douglas. Evelyn sees him, Douglas doesn't. Evelyn continues to kiss for a second or two then breaks. John enters.

Evelyn: Music hall's for dreams though Duggie, not nightmares.

Douglas: Hello John. Last rehearsal then. Straight to the big moment eh? Take your positions. John, you're in the condemned cell. Everything alright up there Mr Berry?

Berry: It appears so.

Evelyn remains on stage to watch the rehearsal. Berry tests the equipment, operating the trap door several times. He takes out his rope and secures it. He lays out his hood and straps. The lighting changes once again, concentrated on the gallows. Berry addresses the audience.

He was perfectly calm, almost indifferent. About four minutes to eight, I was conducted by the Governor to the cell and introduced.

He alights from the scaffold and walks towards Lee

My name is James Berry.

JOHN: How do you do sir?

They shake hands. Berry is guessing his weight.

BERRY: Have you prayed?

JOHN: God knows that I am innocent.

BERRY: Pray that he receives you.

JOHN: I have dreamt that I would not be hung.

BERRY: I am here to do my duty John.

A bell tolls. Berry ties Lee's hands behind Lee. He then leads Lee to the gallows. As he does he quotes from the Burial of the Dead.

'I know that my redeemer liveth, and that he shall stand at the latter day upon the earth and though his body be destroyed, yet shall I see God. Whom I shall see for myself and mine eyes shall behold, and not as a stranger. We brought nothing into the world, and it is certain that we can carry nothing out.'

They are on the gallows. Berry fastens Lee's Legs. Places the white hood over his head. Secures the noose. The bell stops.

Have you anything to say?

JOHN: Drop away

BERRY: *(There is a circus drum roll alongside this)* 'I am the resurrection and the life, saith the Lord; he that believeth in me, though he were dead, yet shall he live.'

The drum roll stops. Berry pulls the lever but the trap doors do not open. He stamps on them, they do not open. The drum beat begins again, getting progressively louder. He takes the noose off Lee. Leads him to one side. Pulls the lever. The doors open this time. Closes them. Brings Lee back to the traps doors, secures the noose, pulls the lever but the doors do not open. Stamps again. They will not open. Takes Lee to one side—they open, stands him on them for a third time–they will not open. In frustration he takes the noose off Lee and the hood. Throws it down. Stares at him. Berry drops to his knees distraught. The drums stops.

DOUGLAS: Very good. You know what we need here. John I need you to say something about Emma Keyse, before you get to the scaffold.

Pause—one beat.

JOHN: Like what?

DOUGLAS: How she was your best friend n all that.

Pause—one beat.

JOHN: 'She would have done anything for me'.

DOUGLAS: Aye. So we all ready for tonight? I think it'll go well.

Exit Douglas with John. Berry tests the trap doors and they appear to be opening when they shouldn't. He looks for Douglas but he's gone. Berry is concerned about the gallows but he also wants to speak to Evelyn, who is exiting.

BERRY: Miss Nesbitt. May I speak with you?

EVELYN: Concerning what?

BERRY: My work.

EVELYN: Oh your work.

BERRY: Mr Fawcett, Douglas, came to see me last night. With an amendment to my contract.

EVELYN: What kind of amendment?

BERRY: I will have to ave his permission to perform at other halls.

EVELYN: You can only hang people for Douglas now?

BERRY: He has offered to increase my turn fee by ten per cent. If I sign up to it, it affects my future as a performer. If I don't, I may not have one.

EVELYN: And what has this got to do with me?

BERRY: You may not feel that we share much common ground, but anyways I'm now an act. And a member of the Variety Artists Federation. Same as you.

EVELYN: Same as me? You think because you're on a bill next to me we're the same. Men threw garlands at me. My songs made them believe they were in love with plain girls. Do you know where I have performed? London. I coulda stayed in London. Coulda gone to America. You, you're not an act.

BERRY: Posters say I am.

EVELYN: Only because Douglas is desperate to keep this place open for some reason. But it'll close soon. And for the better.

BERRY: I doubt it. If what Henry tells me is correct.

EVELYN: And what is that?

BERRY: The bank has provided Douglas with substantial funds. For new acts, for alterations. He has put his house up as surety.

EVELYN: What do you mean?

BERRY: It means he has signed his house/over to the bank.

EVELYN: I know what it means! *(Pause)* Henry told you this?

BERRY: Yes.

EVELYN: When?

BERRY: This morning.

Pause—two beats. Evelyn is furious, is about to walk out, composes herself.

I should let you get on. I just thought you might be familiar with ... such ... clauses.

EVELYN: I don't particularly care where you perform. Sign or don't sign. But if you do–get fifteen per cent out of him. That's the rate. Douglas is selling you short. He does that to people.

Exit Evelyn, Berry turns and looks at the gallows for a moment then exits. A few seconds of silence then the trap doors open all by themselves. Blackout.

A recorded snippet of a music hall song is played between scenes as the show has begun. 'The Man Who Broke The Bank At Monte Carlo' by Charles Coburn.

Scene Nine

The same evening, Evelyn's dressing room, downstage in front of stage curtain. Evelyn has a bottle of sherry on her dressing room table. Enter John. He is wearing a convict uniform for the performance.

EVELYN: John. Nice of you to come. Almost time for the finale.

JOHN: Aye. Few minutes to go yet.

EVELYN: Yes I can still hear Clareece. Though she might've stopped singing a while ago. You must be nervous?

JOHN: I have to keep calm.

EVELYN: Of course. Part of the act.

Pause — one beat.

JOHN: I saw you last night.

EVELYN: I know. Did you enjoy it?

JOHN: I did.

Evelyn pours herself a sherry. She offers John a drink but he declines.

EVELYN: You like the music hall don't you? I saw you talking to the girls, at the back of the stalls. They must have liked talking to such a handsome man.

JOHN: I don't know about that. They'll be watching the act though.

EVELYN: How have the rehearsals been?

JOHN: We have it right now. With the acting and the levers.

EVELYN: And how does it feel, standing on the gallows?

JOHN: I'm ready to do it.

EVELYN: You think God will protect you again, don't you? I've seen acts before that played with death. Some of em pushed their luck too far. But then I always thought, that was what they secretly wanted.

JOHN: I don't intend to do this for very long.

EVELYN: John if you go out on that stage tonight, you will never be anything else. Do you understand? The condemned man's all you'll ever be.

JOHN: I have to do this now.

EVELYN: Why?

JOHN: Because I have said! It's an opportunity for me. Set the record straight.

EVELYN: It's an opportunity for Douglas. That's all. You were in prison long enough weren't you?

JOHN: Aye, working at oakum picking. I'll work no more.

Evelyn takes some money from a bag.

EVELYN: Look, there's enough here for a passage. Take it. Go. Go somewhere where they don't know you.

JOHN: I have a right to perform, don't I? Same as you.

EVELYN: John you know it's not the same.

JOHN: I'm still finding the courage to act alone, but I can do this. I was shown my open grave, but now, I'm gonna be on stage.

EVELYN: It's blood money.

JOHN: No different from your money. This is about you and Mr Fawcett int it? I know. He won't leave his wife for you so you wanna ruin the act, that's all.

John begins to exit.

EVELYN: Good cook was she. That sweetheart of yours?

JOHN: What of it?

EVELYN: I'm not surprised you wanted to keep it a secret. Lizzie, wasn't it?

JOHN: Never you mind bout me and Lizzie.

EVELYN: What happened to the child John? Was it your child?

John approaches Evelyn aggressively.

JOHN: Listen to me. You say another word like that and it will be your last. You hear me.

EVELYN: Her ladyship find out did she?

JOHN: I mean it.

EVELYN: Or perhaps she caught you.

JOHN: Quiet!

EVELYN: With your own flesh and blood!

He takes the sherry bottle and smashes it on the table in anger. Evelyn is terrified. A turn bell rings. John exits.

Dressing room furniture is struck.

Scene Ten

The curtain is raised upon the gallows with Berry standing proudly. Down stage left John is lying asleep on a narrow camp bed. He is wearing a long overcoat over his prison uniform. We hear melodramatic piano music. Douglas stands downstage in a spotlight.

DOUGLAS: Ladies and gentlemen Fawcett's music hall proudly presents to you, two celebrities of the great English murder, no other than John Babbacombe Lee and his very own hangman, Mr James Berry. Please show you're your appreciation as they recreate for us tonight, the incredible story of, The Man They Couldn't Hang!

Douglas runs off stage. Spotlight on the gallows. Then lights dim; a melodramatic piano accompaniment.

The silhouette of a woman in a bonnet on the back wall of the stage (which is Douglas). She screams; then blackout. In the blackout a manikin dressed as an old lady with more than ample blood spillage is placed centre stage.

Lights lift to gloom on John. He begins to stir, the manikin begins to smoke. John awakes and runs over to the body. Returns to his bed and takes a blanket to put out the fire. He beat the body with the blanket.

JOHN: I must break a window to release the smoke.

John rushes off stage and returns with an axe. He imitates breaking a window. Returns to the manikin, kneels.

My poor dear mistress lying on the carpet. A ghastly sight. Her hands are blue, claw like, drawn up in the convulsion of death. Her head almost hacked clean off.

He hugs the body to his breast.

Help! Help I say. Come quick!

Enter Berry wearing a policeman's helmet. John stands, the axe still in his hand.

BERRY: Something foul has happened here.

Berry grabs John by the collar, seizes the axe.

JOHN: She was my best friend, like a mother to me.

BERRY: You are apprehended on suspicion of murder.

Berry drags Lee back to where he was sleeping. John takes off the overcoat and is now in his arrowed convict outfit. Berry mounts the gallows.

JOHN: My trial was a thing so bewildering that it seemed to be nothing but a jumble of words. Til the jury suddenly said "guilty" and the judge passed sentence. I can't quite remember what he said. There was something about place of execution, hanged by the neck … dead … soul. That was all I heard. It seemed as if some far way voice was speaking to me.

Spot on Berry.

Berry: To the ordinary Englishman a murderer is a murderer and nothing else. A vile creature who has taken life and who by law, divine and national must die like a dog. To me, a murderer is a study. The conduct of the condemned in the cell and on the scaffold throws much light upon the various phases of the human character. And to me it has always been an interesting study.

Berry alights from the scaffold and walks towards Lee. En route he steps over the manikin.

Berry: He was perfectly calm, almost indifferent. About four minutes to eight, I was conducted by the Governor to the cell and introduced.

My name is James Berry.

John: How do you do sir.

Berry: Have you prayed?

John: God knows that I am innocent.

Berry: Pray that he receives you.

John: Miss Keyse would have done anything for me. And yet this is the woman they say I murdered.

Berry: I am here to do my duty John.

John: I take Almighty God as my judge. I have spoken the truth.

A bell tolls. Berry ties Lee's hands behind Lee. He then leads Lee to the gallows quoting from the Burial of the Dead and tripping over the manikin.

BERRY: 'I know that my redeemer liveth, and that he shall stand at the latter day upon the earth and though his body be destroyed, yet shall I see God. Whom I shall see for myself and mine eyes shall behold, and not as a stranger. We brought nothing into the world, and it is certain that we can carry nothing out.'

They are on the gallows. Berry fastens Lee's Legs. Places the white hood over his head. Secures the noose. The bell stops.

Have you anything to say?

Pause.

Have you anything to say?

Pause

JOHN: Drop ... away.

There is a drum role. Berry pulls the lever but the trap doors do not open. He stamps on them, they do not open. The drum beat begins again, getting progressively louder. He takes the noose off Lee. Leads him to one side. Pulls the lever. The doors open this time. Closes them. Brings Lee back to the traps doors, secures the noose, John begins to struggle violently.

JOHN: Take the noose off! Unite me!

BERRY: Coughs.

JOHN: Take my noose off. Please!

BERRY: Coughs… Quiet man.

JOHN: Take it off. Please take it off. I'm asking you for mercy now.

John is trying to get his hands free, his head is shaking as if in convulsion. Berry pulls the lever and the trap doors sag. John hesitates then struggles even more, his body writhing.

Let me down, take me off you hear.

John screams and sobs.

I can't do this, please … God in heaven stop this! No, no

Douglas rushes on stage. Wheels the gallows back.

DOUGLAS: Curtain!

The curtain falls, hiding the gallows, enter Evelyn; she sings, without conviction, 'Let The Great Big World Keep Turning', but doesn't get to finish. Booing forces Evelyn to leave the stage prematurely.

Scene Eleven

The curtain lifts. A little while later. Berry, Lee, Douglas and Henry around the gallows. The music hall has finished and emptied for the night. Possibly for good.

DOUGLAS: Do you know who was out there?

JOHN: You have told me Mr Fawcett.

DOUGLAS: The bank manager. Owns this place. My house. Me. I borrow money off him, to pay for you to perform and then you back out.

JOHN: I am sorry.

DOUGLAS: I'll be a laughing stock. Already am. They won't come back. Not now.

HENRY: John try not to look at the audience. Close your eyes if you like.

DOUGLAS: He had a hood on Henry

BERRY: We could put it on from his walk. Tried that once in Carlisle...

JOHN: It is not the audience.

HENRY: Think of the money, the pleasure you could buy with it.

BERRY: Were you worried that something might go wrong?

JOHN: It is not you Mr Berry. I can't perform on the gallows that's all.

DOUGLAS: You signed a contract.

HENRY: If he'd've heard the applause, just once.

JOHN: I won't do it.

DOUGLAS: Why?

JOHN: Cos I murdered Emma Keyse.

Pause — one beat.

DOUGLAS: What?

JOHN: I'm sayin' I killed her. I thought I had to kill her. Like I thought I had to do this.

DOUGLAS: You said you were innocent.

JOHN: I've always wanted to be.

DOUGLAS: Wanted to be …?

JOHN: That's why I've always said I was.

Pause — two beats.

DOUGLAS: Oh … I see … But, wanting and being … that's not … Did you bloody know this?

Henry: He's been saying he was innocent for the last twenty years.

Berry: Only a guilty man would go to such lengths.

Douglas: Hells bells.

Pause — one beat.

They don't know this out there though, do they? Who else knows? No one, so…

John: Not right. I've already been granted mercy once.

Douglas: Not right that I go bankrupt is it?

John: I shan't do it.

Douglas: Alright, say you killed her then. Tell em. They won't care. In fact might be better, mighten it. With a murderer?

Henry: Ruins the whole act that does.

Berry: Not the same at all.

Henry: Needs to be innocent Duggie.

Douglas: Well lie then! You've been lying all this time.

John: I won't.

Douglas: Nobody knows, nobody but us John. That's as good as innocent.

John: I shall go home.

Berry: How am I supposed to make a living now? Have you thought of that?

John: You will have to carry on without me.

Berry: I need to have you to hang.

John: I am going back to Babbecombe.

Douglas: You'll be nobody when you leave here.

John: Maybe that'll be for the best. I shall say goodbye then.

They refuse to acknowledge John, he exits.

Douglas: I'm finished.

Pause — one beat.

Henry: I know, we'll get a double.

Douglas: What?

Henry: Get an actor in, to play Lee.

Berry: It'll never work.

Douglas: If he hadn't've been seen it might. But you put his face in the papers, sold photos of him, walked him on the stage only to disappear, just before the bloody finale!

HENRY: We still have James.

DOUGLAS: Not now. He's just half of a double act that don't exist. Always has been.

HENRY: Still an interesting turn.

DOUGLAS: Who's gonna pay to see him now?

Berry on his feet.

BERRY: It seems that John Lee has sabotaged me for a second time. He will always be a ghost for me.

HENRY: Where are you going?

BERRY: I will have to see if my services are needed elsewhere.

DOUGLAS: Been a pleasure James. Oh and you might like to have a word with me bank manager. Might feel like hanging himself, just don't cock it up this time.

Berry exits.

HENRY I'm sorry Duggie, I thought we'd make a few bob out of em.

DOUGLAS: Did you know Henry?

HENRY: No. No idea. I'm not so sure though.

DOUGLAS: Bout what?

Henry: Jail teaches folk a thing or two. He might be playing us. He's had a bit of limelight, made a few connections and he wants off the gallows, once and for all.

Douglas: He's a bloody con man.

Henry: Tell yourself a lie for long enough, you start to bloody believe it.

Douglas: Yes I know. Doesn't matter to me, matters to the audience. They're all that counts.

Henry: Audience'll forget

Douglas: Audience will go and you know it. *(Pause)* To picture house. Music Hall's finishing. Finished here.

Henry: No. Never finished you.

Douglas: Been thinking bout it. I shoulda sold. Shoulda listened to Evelyn.

Henry: Picture house not entertainment. Moving pictures?

Douglas: Good earners picture houses.

Henry I don't care. People sat staring at an image that can't even hear them laughing.

Douglas: You don't need an orchestra. Just one man and his organ.

HENRY: Sounds like a turn that. *(Pause)* Remember that show we put on, Boxing Day nineteen hundred

DOUGLAS: Twenty turns. I know. Well I can't take the excitement any longer. And it's what the bank wants.

HENRY: Sod the bank

DOUGLAS: Yeah, well I always did.

HENRY: When you're gone, the game's over. You know that.

DOUGLAS: Be a pal and lock up for me.

Hands Henry some keys. Exit Henry. Douglas climbs the gallows. He touches the noose. The lights change and the orchestra strikes up and John and Berry enter, they sing 'Ain't It Grand To Be Bloomin Well Dead' (Campbell and Connelly).

Initially they sing out to the audience

> Lately there's nothing but trouble, grief and strife
> There's not much attraction about this bloomin' life
> Last night I dreamt I was bloomin' well dead
> As I went to the funeral, I bloomin' well said,
> Look at the flowers, bloomin' great orchids
> Ain't it grand, to be bloomin' well dead!
> And look at the corfin, bloomin' great 'andles
> Ain't it grand, to be bloomin' well dead!

They sing to Douglas

> I was so 'appy to think that I'd popped off
> I said to a bloke with a nasty, 'acking cough
> Look at the black 'earse, bloomin' great 'orses
> Ain't it grand, to be bloomin' well dead!
> Look at the bearers, all in their frock coats
> Ain't it grand, to be bloomin' well dead!
> And look at their top 'ats, polished with Guinness
> Ain't it grand, to be bloomin' well dead!

John and Berry are joined by Evelyn then Henry.

EVELYN:

> Some people there were praying for me soul
> I said, "It's the first time I've been off the dole"
> Look at the mourners, bloomin' well sozzled
> Ain't it grand, to be bloomin' well dead!
> Look at the children, bloomin' excited
> Ain't it grand, to be bloomin' well dead!
> Look at the neighbours, bloomin' delighted
> Ain't it grand, to be bloomin' well dead!

HENRY:

> "Spend the insurance", I murmered, "For alack,
> You know I shan't be with you going back"
> Look at the Missus, bloomin' well laughing
> Ain't it grand, to be bloomin' well dead!
> Look at me Sister, bloomin new 'at on
> Ain't it grand, to be bloomin' well dead!
> And look at me Brother, bloomin' cigar on
> Ain't it grand, to be bloomin' well dead!

All four sing out.

> We come from clay and we all go back they say
> Don't 'eave a brick it may be your Aunty May
> Look at me Grandma, bloomin' great haybag
> Ain't it grand, to be bloomin' well dead

They all look at Douglas then exit. Douglas puts the rope round his neck, he tries to reach the lever to hang himself, but he can't. Tries to kick it, can't.

DOUGLAS: Bugger.

The trap doors sag, a couple of inches. Douglas looks down. Curtain falls.

Scene Twelve

A month later. A dressing room off the music hall at the pier end in Scarborough. Evelyn is sitting alone, preparing for her turn. She has her bottle of sherry on the table as usual. Enter John.

JOHN: Miss Nesbitt.

Evelyn turns.

EVELYN: John

JOHN: I hope you don't mind. They said you might have a minute or two. I was visiting and thought I'd come and see you.

Pause—one beat.

EVELYN: How are you John?

JOHN: I dunno, tired I suppose.

EVELYN: I had wondered what you were up to. Sit down.

JOHN: I went to visit my mother, in Babbecombe.

EVELYN: And how is she?

JOHN: She is old. She is the same old mother though.

EVELYN: And what brings you to Scarborough?

JOHN: I been looking for work round here. At the colliery up the road.

EVELYN: Any luck?

JOHN: Not yet. But I got a good record from jail. There's many things I can do. Mr Berry told me you were here.

EVELYN: That's a comfort. It's sweet that you two still keep in touch.

JOHN: We don't really. He's doin a lecture tour at the moment.

Pause — one beat

EVELYN: On what?

Pause — one beat

JOHN: On hanging. For The Abolitionists. He says he's against it now. He asked me to accompany him, but I didn't want to. The act, my act. I shoulda let Emma Keyse rest in peace.

EVELYN: Wasn't your idea.

JOHN: I walked out on Mr Fawcett. Caused him all that upset.

EVELYN: He made his own bed. Can lie in it now.

JOHN: I've been feeling bad about it.

EVELYN: Don't.

John: I know it's wrong that I didn't keep my word, but neither does it seem right that I had to stand between the / jaws of death every night.

Evelyn: What do you want John?

Pause.

John: I needed to come and see you. Explain something.

Evelyn: You don't have to.

John: This past month or so, I did as you said. I took a different name, denied who I was and said nothing bout the hanging. But … then there seemed nothing for me. There's some warmth in being famous. And money. You must know that.

Evelyn: Have you thought … of looking for your child? The workhouse must know something.

John: She'll a full grown woman.

Evelyn: Then she could find you.

John: She might not know. I doubt if Lizzie would have told her. Her mother is all the reason it happened to me.

Evelyn: Maybe they shouldn't've sentenced you to hang John, but you can't blame Lizzie for what you did.

John: No Lizzie always gets away.

EVELYN: They should've hanged you both then?

JOHN: No.

Pause — one beat.

Just Lizzie.

Pause — one beat.

When Miss Keyse walked in on us in the kitchen, calling us beasts and evil and how we were to be thrown out there and then, it was Lizzie's hand that reached for the hatchet and her hand that swung it. When I moved the body upstairs and broke a window I had her blood all over me. The authorities had no interest in anyone but me. By the time it came to my trial, Lizzie was with child. You don't have to believe me Miss Nesbitt but that's how it is. And I don't think it's so wrong that I go back to making my way as The Man They Couldn't Hang. Do you?

Evelyn just stares at him, lights a cigarette.

Enter Douglas.

DOUGLAS: Well I never. Come to scam the pier have yer? You'll not get much outa them. The country bumpkin who knows nowt about the world? Bloody performer you are.

JOHN: I only popped in to see Evelyn.

DOUGLAS: Don't try playing the innocent with me son.

JOHN: I'll say goodbye then.

EVELYN: Goodbye, John Babbecombe Lee.

Evelyn kisses John on the cheek. Douglas to John as he exits…

DOUGLAS: You owe me money you do.

Evelyn makes for the sherry.

EVELYN: The miser returns.

DOUGLAS: Don't you bloody start. In no position to judge me.

EVELYN: I'm in a perfect position, I'm the other side of Yorkshire. What are you doin here anyway?

DOUGLAS: No bloody idea. Bita news that's all.

EVELYN: Shoulda written.

DOUGLAS: What did he want?

EVELYN: Same as you. Brass.

DOUGLAS: He's got a neck full of it.

EVELYN: What's it to you who comes to my dressing room?

DOUGLAS: Get a few visitors do yer?

EVELYN: I've aroused a bit of interest in Scarborough me.

Douglas: I'll bet... From who?

Evelyn: A performer for one.

Douglas: An illusionist is he?

Evelyn: He's a very talented... ventriloquist.

Douglas: *(Douglas laughs)* Go on.

Evelyn: You won't know him.

Douglas: It's alright you can tell me — my lips are sealed.

Evelyn: Used to be an officer in the Navy.

Douglas: Lieutenant / Travis.

Evelyn: Travis.

Douglas: Terrible turn. Doesn't bother me. Has his hand up a sailor's shirt all night.

Evelyn: What's this news then?

Douglas: You wouldn't be interested.

Evelyn: Come all this way haven't yer?

Douglas: I'm getting rid of it. The hall. My hall.

Evelyn: That's an old routine int it?

Douglas: I've a sign outside.

Evelyn: Nobody'll buy it.

Douglas: Gotta buyer. Picture house. Henry's right upset.

Evelyn: Oh well then

Douglas: Says he'll let me have this Yank he's signed up for a tour, does knockabout stuff. Buster somebody or other, bloody stupid name, usual rubbish no doubt.

Evelyn: How much — are picture house offering?

Douglas: Enough. I'm takin it. I'm out. I mean it. I know you won't believe me

A bell rings for Evelyn's turn. She goes to her mirror makes for the door.

I've moved out, I'm in digs.

Douglas takes her by the hand.

Look, I just want you to come back with me, come back and see, while I sign the papers.

The bell again.

Evelyn: I've gotta go.

Douglas: Evelyn, no. There's no point without you. Is there? Haven't we had our last bell? Haven't we … ?

Evelyn and Douglas kiss. The bell rings as the light fades to black.

Curtain

On Being a Writer in Residence in a Prison

Michael Crowley

A residency as a writer in a prison is almost always arranged through the Writers in Prison Network. This is a small Arts Council funded body that established its first residency around twenty years ago. There are currently around fifteen residencies running in England and Wales. Contracts are usually for two years although occasionally some are longer. I'm coming to the end of my third and final year at HM Young Offender Institution (YOI) Lancaster Farms.

There is a familiar uniformity about all prisons; that's the point of them. There is also, it has to be said, a degree of familiarity about prisoners; but each residency will be unique. Institutions do differ, populations are different and so are writers. I am atypical of writers in prison in that I was formerly a youth justice worker, going back into a young offender institution I had visited many times when I was a youth offending team officer. I was writing plays in the day job, gradually getting work produced, until I initially went part time and then left altogether to take up a couple of commissions. The residency came along and I felt like the job was made for me.

The first thing I noticed when I was given a set of keys to Lancaster Farms was how many of my old caseload was on the wings. Boys who I had known from the age of thirteen and younger shouted salutations from cell windows as I walked round the grounds (so much for all those interventions). At least I had a head start in getting established in the institution. For the first eighteen months I was lucky to have another writer in residence alongside me; playwright, journalist and broadcaster Beatrix Campbell. Joint residencies are rare, in our case it worked well. We worked independently yet collaboratively producing anthologies and organising performances of lads' writing together. From the outset it was apparent that there was more than an appetite to write amongst prisoners; there was a need. Prisoners' lives are full of conflict; with the state; with other individuals; with their families and with themselves. They may not necessarily always have great insight or vocabulary, but they have stories in abundance. From my first week to my last month, I was unable to get anywhere near working with all the lads who applied to me.

Today My Hand

Writing at HMP YOI Lancaster Farms

For the most part I began by writing *with* lads. I used warm ups, exercises, storytelling, memory games, but always by the end of the first session, I asked the lads to commit something to paper. Then I set 'homework'. I worked with the same prisoners for as long as I was able to and we were making progress. I worked with some lads for three years. Lifers and long sentence lads were the easiest to work with because their behaviour and attitude tended to be better than those for whom prison is a revolving door. They are also less likely to want to write or read about crime. Both Bea and I were clear that our purpose was to be rehabilitative. To be interested in a prisoner's writing without any regard to how the process will change his thinking and behaviour seemed to us pointless. That meant discussing and writing about specific crimes in detail; grave crimes: the planning and motivation, the commission of the offence; the aftermath on all concerned; its meaning. It is remarkable how little opportunity or requirement there is upon prisoners to discuss the significance of what they have done, particularly in a young offender institution. Young prisoners' writing can often be apocryphal and sentimental; homilies about how they've learnt their lesson or a string of actions that avoid exploring consequences. Lads may have begun writing in that fashion but the project was to always guide them to more concentrated and original expression. And for them to see that other people's stories were just as important as theirs.

> That's all I ever want off people. Their car. I appreciate cars. I understand them. I see the reason why every drop of sweat that has hit the ground during the engineering of a car has done so. I love cars. Everything about them. The way they look, the way they smell, the way they sound, the way they feel, the way they drive, even the way they hurt when they are abused. It's almost as if they talk to me. I can't speak their language though, so I take care of them, look after them, drive them the way they like to be driven, wash them when they are dirty and sad, fix them when they are broken and mad. I can understand why people think I'm crazy. They are right. What was I thinking? Cars don't have feelings; you can't make a car happy. Most illnesses have a cure. I think the only person who can cure this is me and I'm far from a doctor.
> **Roy**

Anthologies were produced with images that steered away from the literal. Often these were launched at a performance in the chapel or the library. Performance in a prison can be fundamental to undermining the pro criminal culture; to establishing a cultural strategy that promotes a different ethic. To begin with, being an audience requires generosity, silence and applause; not found in abundance in a YOI. The preparation to perform, read or act requires discipline and commitment. Performance requires public expression of intelligence and tenderness in hardened young men.

Letters to Myself

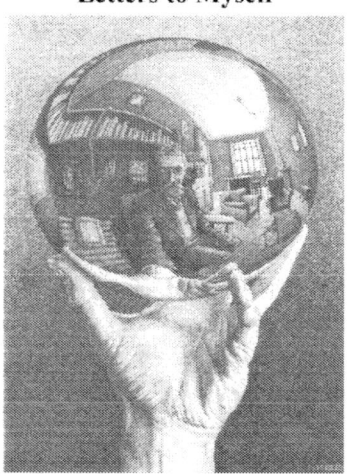

Writing from Lancaster Farms

Most of the drama performed at Lancaster Farms was written by lads under my tutelage. Visiting actors and a director from The Dukes Theatre Lancaster provided more than a little support for performances. Three of the pieces were subsequently produced in showcases of prisoners' work in London. But I also took texts off the shelf that found their own relevance. Shakespeare's Michael Cassio in *Othello* regretting an act of drunken violence, kicking his plastic bottle of blackcurrant across the chapel stage: *Oh God that men should put an enemy in their mouths to steal away their brains.* Steinbeck's black stable hand Crooks in *Of Mice and Men*, forced to live in a barn. I spent six weeks looking at scenes from Timberlake Wertenbaker's *Our Country's Good*. The text became a means of teaching English, Geography and History, the process culminating in workshops with Theatre by the Lake Keswick, who had the play in production at the time. It's more difficult to say (or measure) what lads learn by acting alongside accomplished professional actors, but afterwards appear to have grown in some way. My hope is that *The Man They Couldn't Hang* is used in prisons in a similar way. As a text from which people might learn about Edwardian society, music hall, the actual case of John Babbacombe Lee; as a basis to discuss guilt, redemption, capital punishment, crime and celebrity but most of all, as a play to be performed.

People benefit because it's a way to unlock hidden emotion. It's a way of being understood. It's a way to get out of this world and into another where anything can happen. I've tried to write from a victim of crime perspective, and the truth is, I've never thought like this before. I've never even bothered about people I don't know. I've always thought, if I don't know someone, why should I care? Writing from their perspective makes me think about their lives.
Roy
HMP YOI Lancaster Farms.

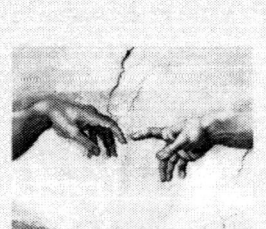

Poems
About Love

From HMP YOI Lancaster Farms

Prison Writing

For a wide selection of titles relating to prisons and imprisonment, crime and punishment visit www.WatersidePress.co.uk

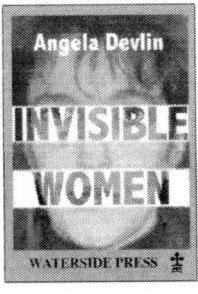

Waterside Press *Putting justice into words*